Teach Your Child to Talk

A Parent Guide

REVISED EDITION

by

DAVID R. PUSHAW

CEBCO | STANDARD PUBLISHING
104 5th Avenue • New York, N. Y. 10011

CREDITS

The quotation on page 46 is from the John Tracy Clinic Language Program *Getting Your Baby Ready to Talk* (1968), John Tracy Clinic, educational center for preschool deaf children and their parents, Los Angeles, California.

Templin Sound Development Norms on page 219 from Mildred Templin, *Certain Language Skills in Children,* Child Welfare Monograph Series #26, University of Minnesota Press, Minneapolis, Copyright 1957, University of Minnesota.

Photographs by William Castellano, Jr.

Illustrations by Ric Estrada

PRINTED IN THE UNITED STATES OF AMERICA

ISBN 88320-993-4

1   3   5   7   9   10   8   6   4   2

This book is dedicated, with love, to the Pushaw tribe, in order of their appearance—Sue, Jim, Bob, John, Tom, Bill, and Maggie.

Acknowledgments

Grateful acknowledgment must first be given to the coauthors of the original *Teach Your Child to Talk:* Norman Collins, Gordon Czuchna, Gary Gill, Gloria O'Betts, and Mike Stahl. During the years we worked together we not only produced materials we all take great pride in; we also had fun. Without question, that work formed the basis for my next five years of work and this revised edition. To the whole gang may I say a special, warm "Thank you" and "I'm proud to have been a part of what we accomplished."

To LeeAnn Lipke, R.N., M.A., for the many, many hours she spent in assisting not only in detailed review and revisions of the text but for her contribution of original materials related to human growth and development.

To Mrs. Ara Cary, M.S.W., Psychiatric Social Worker, former Director of the Grand Rapids, Michigan, Child Guidance Clinic and instructor at the University of Michigan School of Social Work, for her critical, professional review and suggestions.

To my wife, Beverly, for her support in keeping the home fires burning, and making the long nights of writing possible.

To Elaine Misak, my secretary, who struggled to decipher many, many pages of writing and dictation (five drafts!) and turned them into typed, legible copy.

And last, but not least, to the many parents around the country who shared their thoughts with me in workshops and seminars. I thank you one and all.

David R. Pushaw

Foreword

Most of us talk so much and so easily that we take speech and language development for granted. We seldom think about the little child's remarkable achievement when he begins to talk to us. As parents we are delighted to hear the first words uttered by our little one. But we may not realize that he was learning to talk from the very first day of his life.

Most people think of language and speech as being the same thing. However, speech is only one part of language. Language includes all the ways that a person communicates with others and even with himself. It involves paying attention, listening, understanding, speaking, reading, writing, and gesturing.

Human thought cannot grow without language. The child must have names for things and actions and relationships before he can begin to possess his world. With language, his world can become a part of him, extending beyond the immediate present. He can learn to talk about it, think about it, manipulate it, even when it isn't physically there. But first he must learn much about his world through experience. And of course the child's first experiences have no words or language attached to them.

Speech and language development are central to everything else the child will achieve in life. Success in school will depend in large measure on the child's vocabulary and his mastery of the rules of his language. As parents we should not make an exercise of teaching language skills to children. However, we should provide good speech models for the child, and surroundings that will help him to accomplish his tasks of speech and language development. To do this well, we should understand how speech and language develop. We should be glad of any advice as to the right kinds of activities and surroundings to give to our children.

Here is a book, written in simple and interesting fashion, that is made to order for this purpose. In this book you can learn how speech and language develop. You can find a wonderful variety of things to do and materials to use that will provide fun while they help you do the right kind of teaching. Throughout, the author helps you to understand your child's feelings, something that is very important in communicating with him.

This book should be in the home of every ''new'' parent, and it should be available in the office of every physician who takes care of children. *Teach Your Child to Talk* is a treasure chest of ideas for parents who want to help their children achieve the best in language development.

Sylvia O. Richardson, M.D.

Contents

How To Use This Book

Many things that parents do naturally and as a matter of course will help their child learn to talk and to develop speech and language skills. Sometimes, however, parents may unknowingly be putting roadblocks in their child's path to learning. This book is designed to have a direct and positive effect not only on your child's speech and language development but on his total development as well.

The ability to communicate is a desirable goal for authors as well as for parents and children, so I am speaking with you as though we were sitting in your home, talking casually. Even the Appendix sections are informal, but they are full of useful information.

Throughout this book, I will refer to your child as "he." Please accept my apology if you have a daughter. I like little girls. Two of my own children are daughters. Using the word "he" is merely a consistent form of reference.

This handbook has seven chapters tracing a child's development from birth to five years of age, and three general sections entitled "Being a Parent—

How Does It Begin?,'' "If Your Child Has Special Needs," and "One More Time." It may not be necessary for you to read "If Your Child Has Special Needs," but you may find it helpful. The general chapters will help you understand your child's general growth and development. The chapters that specifically relate to his age will give you detailed information about this. All of the chapters organized by age levels are divided into three sections: "Typical Development," "Questions on Development," and "Suggested Activities."

The "Questions on Development" sections will help you decide if all phases of your child's growth and development, in addition to speech and language, are generally on schedule. *Remember, there is no exact age for things to happen. Your baby will grow and develop at a time that is right for him. There are wide differences, all within the range of what is typical.*

These questions are meant only for *you* to answer. Don't ask your child to answer them as he grows older. To use these questions, look at the following table to find the section nearest your child's age:

Answer the questions in the section *nearest* your child's age. If you can answer "yes" to at least half of them, he is probably developing typically. If you cannot, then answer the questions for the next youngest age group. Keep working back until you can answer "yes" to more than half the questions in a section. This will give you an approximate age level of development for your child.

If, according to the "Questions on Development," your child's development level is a year or more behind his actual age, he may need some special attention. Talk to a school psychologist or perhaps your pediatrician if you have questions. Your local school, board of health, or the well-baby clinic of a hospital can usually put you in touch with someone who can help you. You may also get help through United Way information services, a specialist in child development, or a good nursery or day-care center.

Remember that the questions on development represent averages only. Each child is different, and there will be many variations within the limits of what is typical.

The sections on "Suggested Activities" describe specific things to do to help your child develop, but you don't have to follow them down to the last detail. You can easily change or adapt these activities to fit in with your way of doing things.

I have tried to emphasize at all age levels the importance of good parent-child relationships and ways of encouraging them. Many suggestions help create an atmosphere that will make your child feel that it is fun to learn to talk. At the same time, he will learn to like himself and to develop a healthy outlook on life. Also included are many activities that allow a child to learn by seeing, hearing, and feeling. Almost all the activities will help develop skills in muscle coordination, imitating, and learning. At the end of the "Suggested Activities" for the fifth year, you will find items of a somewhat different type that will also be helpful.

The statements in the section "Recognizing Speech and Language Problems Early" will serve as a guide in determining whether your child needs special help in speech and language.

You will find some words in **heavy type** throughout the book. Explanations of these words can be found in the Glossary on page 213.

In the Appendix is a section called "Speech Sounds." It is included to help you understand how sounds are produced. (An important note: *As a general rule, never correct your child's speech from the moment he begins talking until after age six—unless a specialist in speech therapy has told you how to do so.*) You will also find in the Appendix a collection of finger plays to add to the games and plays in the main text of the book. Finger plays aid hand coordination and help build imitation skills, and they are "just for fun," too. The Appendix also includes a list of records for children, and two book lists, one for children and one for parents. These will help you locate good books and records.

This book is meant to help your child learn to talk, and to assist in his total development. The "Questions on Development" are intended to give you a chance to follow his progress. They may alert you to your child's need for more time and attention from you or others, but they are *not* intended as a means of pushing and prodding him to meet certain standards. *Remember, pressure has no place in your efforts to help a child learn to talk or in aiding in his general development.* The intent of this book is not to speed up his development. Instead, it is meant to prevent some of the roadblocks that may, unknowingly, be placed in his way. Learning can be fascinating and fun for you and your child.

Being A Parent—
How Does It Begin?

Is being a parent really so difficult or so different for each of us? Must we find out all we want to know through the long, hard way of trial and error? I don't happen to think so. Yes, there are many things that no one can prepare us for as our children grow and develop. But there is much useful and helpful information we can share with one another.

If there is one activity that helps us develop all of our skills, I feel it is learning to talk. Talking helps us learn about feelings and getting along with people. Through talking, we develop listening skills, seeing skills, thinking skills, doing skills. In this book, ways to develop these skills are presented bit by bit to show you how teaching your child to talk will be fun for both you and your child. It is a guide intended to help—not a program that you *must* follow. It has been developed around your child's natural way of learning, through his curiosity, explorations, trials and errors. Try always to let your child learn the comfortable, natural way. Don't push him or pressure him. Demands for instant or constant success have no place in early childhood.

Where does "parenting" begin? Let's start with your baby's needs as soon as he is born. The feeling of being loved, wanted, cared for—these are your baby's first needs. But how do you let him *know* that you love him, want him, will take good care of him? You can do this with your voice and by the way you touch him. In the beginning, words are not important, but from the moment you hold him, you can say "I love you"; "I want you"; "It's safe to be with me in this strange, noisy world." You do this with the soft, loving tone of your voice and the gentle way in which you soothe him. Your baby is just beginning to live in a world that is new and strange to him. You can build the beginnings of good feelings between you and him with the soft, comforting sounds of your voice and the way you cuddle and hold him. In these ways you let him know that he is loved and wanted. This bright, noisy place he has suddenly come into will take time getting used to. He also needs time to get used to those big, unfamiliar people—his mother and father.

The tone of your voice is more important than your words in these early months after birth—and this is really true all through his growing up. I have often asked new mothers to repeat the items on their grocery shopping lists to their babies as though they were the greatest words of love and tenderness. Try

this and watch what happens. Your baby will slowly begin to "turn on" to what you are saying, as though "apples" and "hamburger" really *were* the most beautiful, loving words.

The way you hold your baby is also very important. Pick him up slowly and gently, making soft, gentle sounds to him. If you keep doing this, you'll soon see little smiles and hear small sounds of happiness. These are called **comfort sounds** (see Glossary). Touch him and hold him firmly but gently. Support his whole body, especially his head. In these ways you let your baby know that he is safe.

A baby needs to get used to being moved. Being picked up and whisked through the air is very strange to him. He was safe and protected by the closeness of the womb before being born. It will take a while for him to get accustomed to being lifted up, even slowly, and then being returned slowly to a bed, your lap, or your shoulder. Pick him up often to cuddle him. He will like the body contact, and so will you. When you move him to give him a bath, change a diaper, or feed him, the *way* you do it can help him

feel secure and build positive feelings between the two of you. Remember: Talk to him in soft, comforting tones. Hold him close. Move him slowly and gently. All these things will help him develop good feelings about himself and you.

You need to learn all about your baby, but he has even more to learn. He must learn all about you *and* all about himself! How will he do this? He will do it through you. Remember, the earliest ways of communicating with him are with sounds and touching. The warm skin contact during breast feeding is a way of saying "I like you" and "You are safe with me." If you bottle-feed him, do so with his skin touching yours. This is one time when you fathers can help out. When you hold and speak to him, your voice will sound much different from his mother's. Your baby will begin to listen to different voices and will learn that he is cared for and loved by different people.

It is important for each of us to have good feelings about ourselves. Building such feelings starts at birth. Your baby is learning now, even though he cannot talk about what he is learning. The feelings you show him will influence the way he feels about you. Let him know that you love him, that he is nice to be with. Make him feel that you are nice to be with, too. Remember, he has so many things to learn—and you are his teacher. But "teaching" doesn't mean that you sit down with your baby and say "Now it's our holding time," "Now it's our sharing time," or "Now it's our speech and language time." You *teach by doing* every moment you are with your baby throughout the day. There are times when just holding and rocking your baby, without any words at all, will teach him all he needs to know just then.

During the next few years, your baby will do much of his learning through play activities. So, start to *play* with him now. Play with him when he makes sounds, smiles, claps his hands, begins to crawl. La-

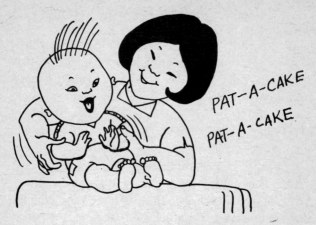

PAT-A-CAKE
PAT-A-CAKE

ter, play with him when he walks, climbs, runs, jumps. Never miss a chance during these early years to join him in his happy, inquisitive world of play, especially if he wants you to. It is hoped that fathers will join in the play as often as possible. All of you have a chance to share wonderful times ahead. Just let them happen. Babies grow quickly into toddlers, and then into preschoolers. They begin to play with other children instead of depending entirely on you as playmates—and before you know it, they're off to school. So enjoy these happy playtimes in his early years.

There are so many ways in which babies can learn, and there are so many things they have to learn. Learning to talk is only one of these. How do you and your baby communicate with each other when you teach your child to talk? Your hands, voice, skin, and face will be the first means of communication you have with him, and will help him begin to learn. Later, his sounds will become words. Then the words will turn into sentences which will help you really understand and know each other. Upon our spoken language we build our reading and writing languages. But always remember, your first ways of communicating will be by touching and the sounds of your voice.

What does your baby have to help him understand you and his new surroundings? First, he has his whole body, which responds to the way you touch and hold him. He also has ears to help him come to know your sounds and words of comfort, love, and caring. He has eyes to see these same things expressed in your face when you are together. As your baby grows, he is developing in many ways, *and all of them are happening at the same time*. He is learning how to see, listen, feel, move about, think, re-

member, and talk. From imitating the sounds you make, he learns to speak words and then to use them in his own sentences as he asks questions and tells you about the things he does while playing or at school. From looking at different shapes and sizes of familiar objects, toys, and puzzles, he later learns to recognize letters, words, and sentences in reading and writing. From his first efforts at creeping and crawling, he eventually learns to ride a bike or fly an airplane. And he will be developing feelings about himself and about others. These are the important

beginnings of his idea of himself as a person. Does he feel good about himself? Does he like himself? Does he feel good about other people most of the time? Does he like and trust other people? Is he usually happy? Developing into the person he will be starts the moment he is born. Learning to feel good about himself, and about you, begins at that moment also.

Many people nowadays are planning their families in advance. Such plans often include adopting a child, or even several children. The information and methods outlined in this book will in general hold for these children as well. However, there are some special considerations to think about.

An adopted child may become part of his new family almost immediately after birth, or when he is but a few months old. In that case, you will be starting as if from scratch, the way you would with your own newborn baby. The younger the child is at adoption, the less relearning he will have to do. But an adopted child is often considerably older, and may come from a cultural background very different from that of his adoptive family. Such a child—one of two, three, four, or more—will have learned a great deal. He may speak a different language, and he may have had experiences and learned customs quite different from those of your household. He must now add to all that he has learned, and will probably have to unlearn much that he has already learned. As you can imagine, this will be very difficult for him. *All* babies and young children have so much to learn in the usual process of growing up, but he will have the additional work of unlearning and relearning.

For such a child, developing· feelings of being loved, wanted, and having a secure place in your family should come first. (This holds true, of course, whether he was adopted in infancy or at a later age.) But if your child was adopted when he was more than a few months old, let the "Questions on Development" go for a while. Later, when he knows and feels he is loved and wanted, you can use them to discover his level of development, and begin to meet his learning needs.

As you read this book, perhaps you will feel that it is addressed mainly to mothers. Fathers are mentioned often, of course, and a father's part in a child's life is a very important one. Nowadays, however, many families have a single parent as head of the household, and this parent is generally the child's mother. While it is best for children to grow and develop from infancy with the help of a mother and a father, this is not always possible. Let us think about being a single parent from a mother's viewpoint.

If you live alone with your child, you can still see to it that your child will have good and necessary relationships with males. How can you go about developing relationships that will help your child? First of all, you may want to turn to your family. Talk to your father, or perhaps a brother, about helping you with your child. Plan regular visits to their homes, or have them come to your home. An understanding friend or neighbor may also be able to supply some of the male needs for your child. It will be up to you to find someone you consider suitable and ask him for help.

When you need someone to take care of your baby while you are out, why not try to find a boy or a young man to do the job? Choose one the way you would choose any responsible babysitter. Talk to friends, get references, talk to his mother, talk to

him. Have him come over ahead of time either the same day or the day before, and show him what you want him to do and how you want him to act with your child. This holds for taking care of a single infant or handling two or more preschoolers.

As a person, you have adult needs, just as your baby has a child's needs. It is natural for you to have male friends and perhaps to form a close relationship with one of them in time. You may then begin to think about marriage or living together. If you do, be sure that you are considering your own needs and feelings as well as your child's. The two are related, but they are also different, and it is easy to get confused about them.

It is not a good idea to form a close relationship with a man and to consider marriage or some other kind of "living together" arrangement just because you think it is "good" for your child. On the other hand, your child should not stand in the way of satisfying your need for a man's love and care.

In any case, you will want to consider your child's feelings about a new man in your life. You may find that your child resents him at first. You will have to find out, too, how the man feels about your child. Spending much time together, before starting to live together, can give all of you a chance to know each other better. Remember, also, that your child may become very attached to a man with whom you spend much time. If you later separate, the man's absence may be painful for the child.

These are all very complicated matters. You may feel you need counseling assistance to help understand and resolve your problems. Your local department of mental health, public psychological services, and social service agencies are available to provide this help, often at very low cost.

It is possible, then, for a single parent to provide a child with the male and female relationships he needs to help him grow and develop. It will take doing on your part, but it is possible to remain a single parent and provide for the needs of your child.

In many discussions with parents, conversation has centered around two important topics—*child management* and *discipline*. At first, many parents think these terms have the same meaning. But as discussions continue, parents decide the two terms have quite different meanings. Child management is regarded as a broad, overall way of helping a child learn to get along with others. It means helping a child learn about rights—his own as well as those of others. In learning about rights, he will also learn that there are limits to what he may do. The first of these limits are concerned with his own health and safety. (For example, you put him to bed at a regular time,

and don't let him near an open stairway.) Discipline, on the other hand, is thought to mean using such methods as spanking, scolding, or punishing to train and teach. Child management is a more positive method than discipline. It will be better for helping your child grow and develop.

Child management is essential in teaching your child to talk. It begins with a baby's first cry. Of course, every baby knows how to cry; nobody has to teach a baby that. Crying is the only way he has to let you know about his needs. But crying also plays an important role in his growing, development, and learning to communicate. A certain amount of crying is necessary for the development of his vocal cords, lungs, and chest muscles. However, if he cries a great deal, he will make fewer sounds like those used in talking. If you manage to keep him dry, warm, well fed, and happy most of the time, he will have a better chance of making more comfort sounds. These early comfort sounds will lead to making other kinds of sounds, and will eventually help him say his first real word.

Crying is, therefore, necessary in learning to talk. It is the first step in communication. Child management begins with *how* you respond to your baby's cries. In time, you will come to know his cries as you take care of his needs, and will develop a schedule that meets your needs as well as his. To do this, *you need not always respond to all cries instantly*. You can "teach" him that you will talk to him or pick him up often when he is happy and contented—more

often than when he is crying. This will lead to a happier baby, a more convenient schedule, and more sounds that will help him learn to talk. So you see, good child management and teaching your child to talk are related. (Because good child management is so important, you will find more on this subject in the chapter "One More Time," on page 205.)

A final word: Being a parent is wonderful, exasperating, simple, complicated, easy to do, impossible to do. . . . This book was written to share with you the experiences of many mothers and fathers, so that all of "parenting," including teaching your child to talk, will be more fun and more meaningful for you and your child.

If Your Child Has Special Needs

Perhaps you are wondering why a chapter about children with special needs appears before the chapters that discuss typical learning and activities at different age levels. There is one simple, basic reason, and it will reaffirm what parent after parent knows and feels—that these children are *children* first, even though they do have special needs.

To all parents who are now helping children with special needs to cope with the world in which they live, I would like to begin with this single message, the most important I can possibly share with you:

All children should be given the opportunity to experience every growing and developing adventure that takes place during that very special time called childhood.

This means that early diagnosis is a very important factor in starting a preventive program. If your baby's impairment or problem is diagnosed at an early stage, you can get started on teaching programs which will help prevent delays in his total learning process. Many delays can be prevented by making sure he has a full range of experiences matching his capabilities. Nothing should be withheld, though you may have to modify your ways of sharing things with him.

Almost all the ideas, suggestions, and helps in this book can and should apply to your child. It is not impossible. Some things may be more difficult than others and a few—just a very few—may not be possible. In limited ways, however, I feel all are worth trying. If you are in doubt as to the capabilities or limits of your child, try each suggested step gently and easily—but do try. Let your special child experience life. Overprotection will not help him get ready for adult life. All too often, this is one of the main problems I have to work through with parents. Parents and teachers sometimes think they are helping a child by doing things for him—for example, carrying a blind child rather than letting him learn to creep and crawl, or not talking to a deaf child because he can't hear, or dressing and feeding a child who does not have the use of one or more limbs. In fact, these overprotective attitudes and actions may add *more* delays to a child's growth and development, perhaps even turning small problems into bigger ones. Your child will imitate your words, actions, and feelings. If those words, actions, and feelings are positive ones, then he, too, will respond with positive words, actions, and feelings. Overprotection may lead to emotional problems as well. I know from personal as well as professional experience how difficult it can be for a parent to keep working with an impaired child at the tasks that are set for him to accomplish. But if professional diagnosis has shown that your child has a specific impairment or problem, then for his sake, set realistic goals and *try*.

Please remember that if your child is struggling simply to survive because of some health problem, especially very early in his life, there may be delays in his speech and language development as well as in all other areas of growth and development. The more difficult or more complex the impairment, the more challenging it will be for you to adapt these suggestions so as to give him the experiences that will help him grow and develop. There may be times when your patience will be sorely tried. There may be many moments of frustration for both you and your child. At such moments you will find other people ready and eager to offer assistance. Many persons can and do feel deeply about you and your child, and are likely to try to put themselves in your place. They may be sympathetic and well-intentioned, but unless someone has experienced the constant twenty-four-hour responsibility of caring for a child with an impairment, it is impossible to match the feelings and commitments you as a parent face. I had always felt that I understood such a responsibility as well as any parent, but it wasn't until a serious automobile accident affected one of my teenage sons that I came to understand the depth of the feelings that develop between parents and a child with an impairment. Let me share with you a message given me long ago: "Let him try. Help him try. Make sure he has a chance to try—so that he may experience life! If you can do this, you can give him nothing greater."

In our look at children with special needs, we will talk about children who have impaired vision, hearing, or other physical or health-related impairments; about children having mental or emotional impairments; and about hyperactive children.

For children with impairments, many speech and language difficulties are *learned* as a result of getting off to the wrong kind of start. Correction of these problems requires tremendous effort, and can be agonizingly slow or painfully frustrating. And so, this chapter is placed here in order to help avoid, eliminate, prevent, or reduce problems that are learned.

Some children have impaired vision, hearing, or other physical or health-related impairments. Some have severe emotional problems. Some are mentally retarded, and are unable to learn at the same pace as others. This book is aimed at assisting *all* parents to help their children grow and develop. Parents and teachers of children with special problems have often spoken to me about how they have been helped by the first edition of *Teach Your Child to Talk*. Here are some of the things they have said: "We are using the developmental scale as a guide for parents whose children are retarded because it gives them realistic guidelines and helps take pressures off their children." "We use it for our child who is deaf because he needs exactly what our hearing child needs, *plus more*." The *plus more* feeling is what this chapter is all about.

As we talk about these children, four words are offered to help you and your child: Be patient . . . don't pressure.

THE CHILD WHO HAS IMPAIRED VISION

Time and again, the words "learning to see" will appear in this book. If a child cannot see at all, or not very well, his "seeing" skills may develop slowly—but they *will* develop. He will learn as much as a sighted child—but differently, for he will count on all his other senses to do the job. Keep on talking to your baby—and don't use words that are different from those you would use in talking to a child with normal vision. In fact, talk more! Let him "see" with his ears, his hands, and the rest of his body. As his speech and language development begin, he must *hear* explanations for everything. Learning to listen takes on new importance, so that he can identify sounds and their locations. Try not to change your style of talking by avoiding words like "see" and "look," because your tone and inflection, when you use these words, will help him understand what is being said. If possible, do not change the positions of the furniture in your home. Teach your baby how to crawl around, over, and under the various pieces. When he walks, teach him how to find his way through the house by feel and by sounds. (Going barefoot indoors and, when possible, outdoors, will help him learn by feeling.) Keep things that make noises—the radio, television, clocks that tick, a mixer in the kitchen—in the same places, and he will be able to tell where he is and move through the house by their sounds. Make sure steps are closed off with gates. Later, when he has mastered stair-climbing, it will not be necessary to close them off. (He definitely should learn how to walk up and down stairs at the right age for this.) When you go outside with him, explore that part of his world just as you did in the house, explaining every inch of territory—your yard, the street, and the sidewalk. Remember, like any other small child, he needs to explore in order to learn.

THE CHILD WHO HAS IMPAIRED HEARING

If you have read the preceding unit on the child with impaired vision, you have probably guessed that you will concentrate on seeing and touching if your child's hearing is impaired. Even the most profoundly deaf baby may be fitted with hearing aids to help him "feel" sounds. As an assist to learning, with or without hearing aids, talk, talk, talk, *talk* to him. He will learn a great deal from your facial expressions when you do. Show him things and use gestures more than you usually would, to help him learn to imitate you. He may struggle to understand words and sentences, so talk to him as you do things, whether it is changing diapers or playing games, and be sure to combine words and actions over and over. Let him "feel" sounds as much as possible. Have him touch your throat with his hands when you are imitating his comfort sounds, babbling, and words. Let him feel the vibrations of a kitchen mixer or vacuum cleaner, or of the radio or television when music is playing. These are other ways of helping him know about sounds. Let him experience many listening activities, no matter how simple or difficult they may seem. Just remember to help him along by showing and touching as he "listens" and learns.

THE CHILD WHO IS PHYSICALLY IMPAIRED OR HAS A HEALTH-RELATED IMPAIRMENT

Visible Physical Impairments

Impairments that can be recognized by sight include **muscular dystrophy, spina bifida, hydrocephalus, cerebral palsy,** and **microcephaly** (see Glossary). These will probably be recognized immediately by a physician. I am sure you will then receive prompt medical counseling and assistance. Ask for counseling and assistance regarding your child's development as well. Many hospitals have teams of professional workers, including educators, who will plan a program designed just for you and your baby, to be carried out in your home.

If you do not have a source of such medical assistance near you, make every effort to find someone who can help. Your local health department will have doctors and nurses to turn to. A law now in effect in Michigan requires local schools to provide programs for every child known to be impaired, no matter what his impairment, from the moment of birth on. Other states may also have such a law. For additional help, be sure to check with your community's schools, as well as with agencies such as the March of Dimes Foundation, Muscular Dystrophy Foundation, and the United Cerebral Palsy Association.

When working with children having these impairments, it will be entirely natural to use the suggestions in this book, especially the hearing, seeing, and touching activities. But be aware of your child's physical limits. Be sure to watch for signs of his being tired, such as crankiness or lack of interest, especially when you try activities that involve muscle coordination. The reminder *"Do not push, force, or make demands"* is doubly important here. *Do* help him try—but *don't* make demands.

Nonvisible Physical Impairments

Diabetes, epilepsy, and **hypoglycemia** (see Glossary), as well as heart defects and some other rare diseases, cannot be recognized by sight. In time, however, there may be a related condition, such as an epileptic seizure or retarded growth, that can be observed.

Early diagnosis is once again the key to planning a program that will prevent greater problems from arising. The earlier you are aware of your child's problem and limits, the sooner you will know what he may or may not be able to do. For instance, if you find that he tires easily, then you know that you must plan many short sessions for doing things together. At first, an activity such as creeping and crawling may be a big task and he may not want to do very much of it. That's when you'll have to coax him and make it a little more interesting, so he will try. The hardest thing to do may be to force yourself to make him try. You may feel sorry for him, thinking that some of the things are too hard or too tiring for him to do. But for his sake, it is important that you and he keep on trying until you *learn* his limits, instead of just guessing at what those limits are.

THE CHILD WHO HAS CEREBRAL PALSY

The muscles of a baby with cerebral palsy will be

affected both in their growth and control. Once more, early identification is important. You should receive help from your doctor and a professional such as a physical therapist in planning a teaching program for him.

As you follow the suggestions and activities in this book, the muscle activities should receive your extra efforts as your child grows and develops. It will help if you add to and adapt all of the muscle activities that are outlined here from birth to age five. At the same time, do not overlook learning to hear, see, touch, and feel.

If you know that you should expect delays in development because of impairments, this should help you set realistic goals for your child. This means paying close attention to *how he is doing* and not only to *what he is saying*. I remember a severely impaired 18-month-old child with cerebral palsy who, in addition to his almost complete lack of muscle control, also had a vision problem for which he had to wear glasses. He made very few sounds and could not creep or crawl, yet he could get his mother's attention whenever he wanted it. His little arm would come up slowly and haltingly. His fingers would wrap around his glasses and he would tug them off. As quickly as his mother noticed, she would rush over and take the glasses from him, put them back on him, all the while scolding in a loving fashion: "No, no, no, Tommy. Tommy mustn't do that. Now you leave your glasses on." While gently scolding, she would be patting him, rearranging his clothes, or running her hand through his hair. I saw Tommy do this at least a half dozen times during a morning session of observation. Because he was so quiet and he was so little trouble, he tended to be overlooked in his busy home. Tommy wanted attention and, in spite of his great limitations, knew how to get it.

Learn to watch and really see what is happening with your child. It does take time. But if you do this, you will eventually know the difference between those things he has real trouble doing and those things he doesn't want to make the effort to do.

THE CHILD WHO IS MENTALLY IMPAIRED

Children known to be mentally impaired should have the opportunity to take part in all the activities and experiences described in this book. This will help them reach their highest levels of development. It also means you are providing them the best "parenting" support you can give. I must say a special word of caution, however, about the demands and pressures that can be placed on mentally impaired children.

Most of us have goals and expectations for our children, and it is often very difficult to accept some realities. In all my teaching, I have always tried to be optimistic and I have tried to share my philosophy with you throughout this book. You are asked again and again to try to help your child develop to the greatest possible extent. This is not the time to make an exception to the rule. However, it is possible that in your deep care and concern for him, you may lose sight of him as an individual. Are you demanding for his sake, or for your sake? Are the goals you set your goals, or goals he can reach? Are they realistic, or are they too much? If you're not sure, perhaps the questions on development in each chapter will help you take a realistic look at what your child's limitations and capacities may be. *Please don't lose sight of him as a person.*

THE CHILD WHO IS EMOTIONALLY IMPAIRED

Sometimes, no matter how hard we try to do "all the right things," there are days when nothing seems to go the way we think it should. There are times when you may ask yourself "Why does he act like that?" If you believe your child has severe emotional problems, or if he has been diagnosed as having such problems, you may ask yourself, "How did this happen?" Although you know that you have done your very best to help your child grow and develop, you may feel that you have failed him in some way. But there are other things that must be taken into consideration. The experiences you give your child are only part of the answer to the questions "Why?" and "How?" A child's physical and mental makeup are very complex. There are some areas, such as inherited factors, over which you have no control at all. While we may know much about young children and how they develop, there are still many unknown areas, especially the processes that take place within the mind.

When the development and use of the learning and emotional processes are completely understood, it will be possible to offer guides that are much more specific and helpful. Until that time, only general guidelines for growth and development, such as the ones in this book, may be offered.

Please remember this: As parents, we cannot take *all* the credit for the acceptable ways in which a child grows and develops, any more than we should accept *all* the responsibility when he has problems in his growth and development.

If you feel your preschool child is emotionally impaired, seek help—the sooner the better. Turn to your school, doctor, department of health, department of mental health, or some other well-known agency in your community. Early intervention offers the best possibility for accurate diagnosis and treatment to overcome this impairment.

THE CHILD WHO IS HYPERACTIVE

Most children at one time or another are busy, busy, busy. They "get into" all sorts of things. They are always on the go, whether inside the house or outside. They rush from one toy to another. They make any room in the house a shambles in five minutes. They argue with you, a brother, or a sister long after the arguments should have ended. Most children will do some or all of these things now and then. However, if your child does them frequently, persistently, or most of the time, you may have a youngster who is **hyperactive** (see Glossary).

Signs of hyperactivity may show up as early as the crib years. An infant may be fussy, colicky, restless, and demanding. He may not seem to like being cuddled or comforted. He may cry a great deal, have a poor sleeping schedule, move around a lot, or take a long time to feed. Such a baby may be hyperactive.

If your child is hyperactive, *patience* will be your main requirement. His short attention span will need to be stretched out. Find out what he likes. Then you can concentrate on that for longer periods of time. He may like his bath, or certain games, or certain kinds of music coming from a radio. As he gets older, be ready to do things over and over again without saying "This is the tenth time I've shown you how." He needs extra rewards and encouragement when he is doing something right. The best rewards are hugs, smiles, little pats, and words of approval such as "I like that," "You did that well.

Try to *plan out* whatever you do together, and let him help in the planning. Planning does not have to be complicated. Making a shopping list together is planning. Letting him help you make sure his clothes are ready when you go somewhere is another way of planning. He will be helped through planning, repeating, and rewarding all that he does from early infancy onward.

Please remember that a child is a child for such a short time. Yes, some of them may have impairments, but that does not change the fact that first of all they are children, and that we should help them know as many joys and wonderful times as possible through all their days of childhood.

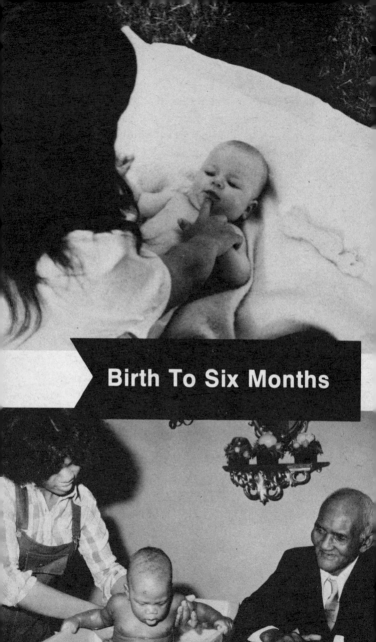

Birth To Six Months

TYPICAL SPEECH AND
LANGUAGE DEVELOPMENT

Learning to talk begins when your baby first cries. Early crying is automatic; it just happens. When a baby cries, muscles tighten all over his body, including those muscles in his throat that close and open the vocal cords. He takes a breath, and as he lets the air out, it causes his vocal cords to vibrate, making voice sounds, including the sound that we call crying. Your baby discovers very early that crying can be useful. He learns that somebody will eventually come to take care of him if he cries. He will gradually associate crying with the attention he gets. His simple cry for help is the first kind of communication you and your baby understand—even though you may not like to hear him practice, especially at three o'clock in the morning!

Your baby learns how to cry in different ways. His crying may be loud or simply a whimper. He may cry in a high or low pitch. He can produce a long, sustained cry or shorter outbursts. After a mother listens to different kinds of crying for a few months, she usually can tell just by the sound of a cry whether her baby is hungry, wet, tired, or cranky. Her response helps him understand that his crying can mean different things to his mother. It is his first step in learning to communicate.

However, a lot of crying is not good for a baby, even from the standpoint of speech development alone. He makes more sounds like those used in actual speech when he is not crying. He makes the first of these by accident. Like early crying, these sounds are the result of unintentional muscle changes as he breathes out or as he breathes in. The enjoyment he gets from making them encourages him to make even more. Since they are usually made when a baby is comfortable, they're called **comfort sounds** (see Glossary).

During the first eight months, your baby is able to understand you through the sound of your voice and by means of the gestures you use. (Remember, he doesn't know the meanings of words.) The things that people do with their voices are called **voice gestures** (see Glossary). We can make our voices soft and pleasant or loud and harsh. We change our voices quite naturally as we talk, without even thinking about it. Babies understand us by what we do with our voices as well as by our hand motions, facial expressions, or other body motions. The tone of your voice and the movements you make show your feelings, and mean more to a baby at this time than the words you say.

Remember, your baby has been in a warm, quiet, protected place for a long time before being born, and this is a new, strange world for him. The way you touch him, hold him, carry him, and speak to him will help him learn to like you, to feel good about himself, and to develop self-confidence. These feelings begin with being cuddled, nuzzled, talked to, smiled at, and being carried gently and slowly. As you carry him, he will also begin to develop his muscles when he arches his back, cranes his neck, or peeks over your shoulder.

Within his first few months, he will be able to see well enough to notice and "talk" to a mobile or other

toy hung over or alongside his bed. Don't be surprised if he seems to wiggle expressively when he is "talking" to it. He is starting to see differences in colors, shapes, and sizes. Even though he doesn't know the words for what he sees, he is beginning to notice these differences and respond to them.

Listening from a very early age is very important for speech and language development, and is also very important in learning to read. Listening means learning to tell the difference between sounds. Eventually, it means hearing the difference when someone says "thoap" instead of "soap," and knowing that the letter "b" stands for the sound "buh," and that "p" stands for "puh." Learning to listen means being where the sounds are. It means spending time near one's mother and father. It means being where the family action is, not tucked away in a quiet bedroom most of the time. It means having a chance to listen to different voices, household noises, and all sorts of sounds that are all around us.

Once again, let me remind you that the first communication between you and your baby takes place when he cries and you react to his cries. Child management begins with *how* you react to his cries. He may cry when he is hungry, tired, wet, uncomfortable, or lonely. Your response to his cries will help him find out that there are times for feeding and sleeping as well as times for cuddling and playing. Good child management begins with setting schedules for eating, sleeping, and playing. Remember, however, that all such schedules are adjustable. They should suit your needs as well as your baby's. Getting started may be hard on you and the rest of the family for a while, but within a few weeks you should be able to establish a schedule that is satisfying to you and your baby.

QUESTIONS ON DEVELOPMENT

You and your baby are just beginning to get used to each other. You both have much to learn. Also, no two babies develop in exactly the same way and at the same rate, so it is hard to say what is typical for babies at this age. Do not become alarmed if you answer "no" to more than half of these questions. Just use the questions as a guide for figuring out the kinds of activities you might want to do as you and your baby get to know each other.

BIRTH TO THREE MONTHS: General

1. Does your baby tighten his muscles when you pick him up?
2. Does he make noises when he's not crying (throaty noises, grunts, or sighs)?
3. Does your baby cry when he's wet or hungry?
4. Does your baby smile when he hears the sound of your voice, when you come near him, or when you pick him up?
5. Does he seem to enjoy having people near him, especially his mother?
6. Does he make a lot of different kinds of sounds?

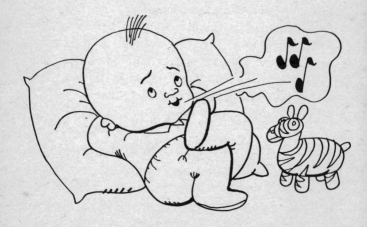

7. Does he smile, coo, or blow bubbles when you smile, talk to him, or come near him?
8. Does he sometimes reach out toward you?
9. Does he express pleasure by making sounds?
10. Does his cry sound different when he's hungry, uncomfortable, or tired?
11. Does he open his mouth for his bottle or the breast?
12. Does he raise his head when he is lying down?
13. Can he hold his head up for four or five seconds?
14. Does he hold a rattle or toy for a few seconds?
15. Does he follow a rattle or toy with his eyes when you move it from side to side?

BIRTH TO THREE MONTHS: Hearing

1. Do loud and strange noises startle or interest him?

2. Does he turn his head toward a sound or react to it in some other way?

3. Does he seem to hear the sound of footsteps approaching his crib?

4. Does he stop crying or react in some other way when he hears his mother's voice before he can see her?

FOUR TO SIX MONTHS: General

1. Is he making a greater variety of sounds?
2. Does he smile and laugh as he makes sounds?
3. Does he show interest in people or objects around him?
4. Can he sit propped up for ten or fifteen minutes?
5. Does he roll over?
6. Does he seem to talk to people around him by making sounds?
7. Does he pronounce syllables (like "bee," "da," "ma," "pa") even though they do not seem to have any particular meaning?
8. Does he make voice sounds when he's alone?
9. Does he seem to know there's a difference between strangers and the people he sees every day?
10. Does he use his voice to:
    (a) get attention (like demanding his bottle)?
    (b) show he dislikes something (like certain foods or loud noises)?
    (c) show enthusiasm (when he sees his bottle or hears his mother's voice)?
11. Does he like to say one syllable, such as "da, da, da, da," over and over again? (See **babbling** in Glossary.)
12. Does he make sounds in response to his toys?
13. Does he make sounds when looks in a mirror?

14. Does he seem to know when others are talking in a friendly or angry way?
15. Does he use combinations of sounds (such as "ma-ba" or "pa-wa") as if they mean something important?
16. Does he sit and hold up his head without support?
17. Does he hold his head steady when you carry him?
18. Does he arch his back when you carry him?
19. Does he look at his hands?
20. Does he reach for something offered him?

AT SIX MONTHS: Hearing

1. Does he turn toward familiar sounds (like that of a dog barking)?
2. Does he try to imitate sounds other people make?

After answering these questions, you may feel anxious; a lot of parents do. Just remember that *these questions on development represent averages only. Each child is different, and there will be many variations within the limits of what is typical.*

If you are concerned about your child's development, talk to your pediatrician or a school psychologist. You can also go to the well-baby clinic of a hospital or the local health department to get answers to your questions. You may find help through United Way information services, a specialist in child development, or a good nursery or day-care center. You will probably be reassured, but if something *is* amiss, you will be getting early help for your child.

SUGGESTED ACTIVITIES

Emotional Development. The way you talk to your baby, the way you treat him, and the way he gets along with other people in the family are very important in his learning to talk. The way you talk to your baby will influence how he thinks about himself. He will learn to like himself better if you talk to him with a soothing voice that lets him know he is part of a secure and loving home. Hold him close; show that you enjoy being with him. Teach him that you and the rest of the family are fun to be with. Help him learn to like other people. According to one expert in child language development, "A baby's great need early in life is for love, affection, and good physical care. Being loved and cuddled helps a baby learn to live in the world."

Before your baby will talk, he must first discover that talking is something he wants to do. Do things that will convince him it is worth the effort he has to make. Hold your baby and let him hear friendly, affectionate talk. This will help him associate speech and language with something pleasant and enjoyable.

Imitation. Imitation is very important in learning how to talk. Learning to imitate starts now. You can easily make a game of teaching your baby to imitate. The first step is to copy the things *he* does. Don't expect him to imitate you, at least not yet. Imitate his smiles, his movements, and the kinds of sounds he makes, even little whimpers. If he says "mmmmbah," then you say "mmmmbah." This will help him develop an interest in imitation and encourage him to imitate your sounds and other sounds later on. Do not think of this as **baby talk** (see Glossary). When your baby is at this age, your repeating his sounds will help him develop imitation skills.

Basic Talking Times. Talk to or imitate your baby when you dress, feed, bathe, or change him, or when the two of you just decide to sit down and "chat." Be sure he is able to watch you talk and can hear you during these times. Remember to keep your gestures and the tone of your voice consistent and reassuring. These times provide opportunities for your baby to feel good about talking.

Learning How to Listen. Let your baby hear as many different sounds as possible to help him develop his listening skills. When you leave him alone in his crib, he will be soothed by such things as the tinkling of wind chimes, a clock that ticks quietly near his bed, or soft music from a radio, record player, or tape recorder. Make sure he's near you when you are cleaning the house, washing dishes, or talking to friends. This way, he will have a chance to sort out sounds and voices and know that there are many different things to hear and know about. Let him play with several rattles, each one with a different sound. These are usually a baby's first sound toys, and they can help him learn to listen. He already has the ability to do this, so give him the chance to use it.

Pictures and Crib Mobiles. Because your baby spends a lot of time in his crib, give him interesting things to look at. Put brightly colored pictures on nearby walls. They don't have to be expensive. An older child's art work or pictures cut from magazines are fine. Just make sure they are bright.

Hang mobiles near or from his crib. (A mobile is a group of lightweight objects suspended on strings or wires so that they balance and are easily set in motion.) To make a mobile, cut out a few triangles, rectangles, and circles of different sizes from boxes of different colors. Paste, glue, or staple pieces of the same shape back to back, or color the plain side of each piece—the brighter the colors, the better. (Note: A baby's first mobile should be made mostly of round objects, because babies seem to "talk" more to things that are round.) Take several jar lids and punch holes in them along the rim. (It's a good idea to paint the tops of the lids in bright colors.) Tie two coat hangers together, using strong thread or string (see Picture A).

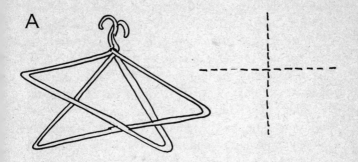

A

Now you are ready to put the mobile all together (see Picture B).

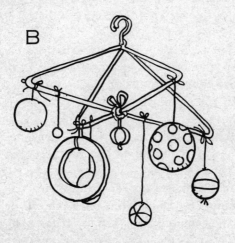

B

Make sure your baby cannot reach the mobile

*when you hang it over or beside his bed. Once he
learns to stand up, move it out of his reach.* Change
the mobiles now and then as he gets older so he will
have a variety of shapes, sizes, and colors to look at.
Studies show that the more interesting and attractive
his surroundings are, the more a baby learns, and the
more he learns, the more he wants to learn. As your
baby becomes aware that things have different
shapes, sizes, and colors, he is *beginning to see.* At
the same time, he is beginning to "talk." If you talk
along with him now and then, he will like it, and will
make more and better sounds.

Rocking Chair. If possible, use a rocking chair
when holding your baby. It provides a combination
of motion, touch, and comfort for the baby and some
moments of relaxation for a tired mother or father. A
baby's sense of touch is highly developed. At this
early age, he will learn more effectively by touching
and by being touched. Holding your baby close, as
when you're feeding him, gives him a chance to
explore your face with his fingers and to observe
your face closely as you talk to him. It is *very* important that you give him physical warmth and affection
when he is very young.

Touching, Holding, and Carrying. Touching, holding, and carrying really go together, but because of
some important things that happen when you do
them, let's look at them separately.

Touching. Touching your baby is a whole body
process—yours and his. When you feed him by either
breast or bottle, the touching of skin on skin will feel
good to both of you. When you change his diaper or

give him his bath, your gentle touch on his body will make him feel good. When you add comforting sounds and let your face show love, you are helping him learn to like himself as well as learning to like you. Learning to like himself is the beginning of developing self-confidence.

Holding. Remember that for about nine months your baby has been held and kept in a warm, protected, dark place. Now he has to get used to light, space, noise, and even breathing. When you pick him up to hold him, make sure you pick him up slowly and with plenty of support for his head. Slow movements are easier for him to get used to; they build his trust in you. If you pick him up to raise him over your head, do it *slowly,* holding him firmly, giving him a reassuring smile, and talking to him gently and softly as he moves. If you do it this way, later on he will be able to handle roughhousing and will really enjoy being tossed in the air.

Carrying. We usually think of carrying a baby around in the "burping" position, up on a shoulder, but there are many ways to carry him. It's important for him to be carried in different ways because this is another "starter." It's helpful for his large muscle development, and as times goes on he will get a different view of the world instead of always looking over your shoulder and seeing where he's been. Try carrying him in a packsack or infant seat, and sometimes have him facing forward as well as back. This will cause him to adjust his body to the way you move and bend. These motions will help those large muscles begin to develop. When you are in a hurry

and hoist him up to your hip, try to remember to use the right hip as well as the left, even if it ties up your good right hand. The positions on either hip will have him using his muscles a little differently.

Toys and Learning by Touching. Learning by touching different things is very important. It is different from being touched. To get an idea of what it's like, close your eyes, touch several things, and see if you know what they are. Learning by touching will help your baby learn to talk, and will also help him get ready to learn to read. It will give you things to talk to him about, too. You can help your baby learn by offering him all sorts of things that are of different shapes and sizes, and that feel smooth, rough, soft, hard, furry, or bumpy. Your baby should play with a good many small toys, but not too many at one time. Give him soft rubber or plastic toys; rattles and other smooth-surfaced toys too large for him to swallow are good. Look around your house for plastic bowls, dishes, or containers—the more different shapes the better. Be sure to give your baby a chance to learn by touching as well as by being touched.

Cradle Gym. You can buy a cradle gym or make one yourself by stretching a wide piece of elastic across your baby's crib and then attaching smooth-surfaced toys or objects to it. Include a favorite rattle, a rubber ball—and look around the house for such things as empty large-sized thread spools. Give him some objects to grab, pull, and bat around. Change them now and then for variety. *Be sure they are too large to swallow, and that they are securely fastened.*

Child Management. Good child management begins with answering your baby's cries and with taking care of his needs. Two things that will help are:

1. *A regular bedtime.* Your home should be pleasant and relaxed at bedtime. Rock your baby, sing to him, and get him in a good mood for sleeping. Sing lullabies to him or make up little songs yourself, even if you can't carry a tune. It doesn't matter to him. Keep his bedtimes consistent, putting him down when he is tired, but also when you decide he should nap or rest.

2. *Sensible feeding schedules.* Learning to eat is another brand-new experience for your baby. He must get used to food, whether he is bottle- or breast-fed. Try to be relaxed at his feeding time. It will help him enjoy eating. Remember, work out a feeding schedule that suits you as well as meets his hunger needs.

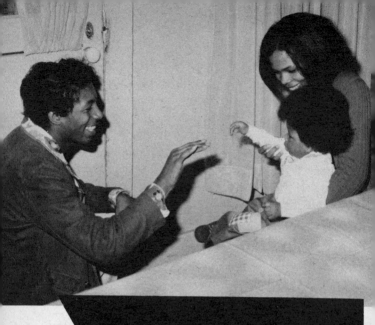

Six To Twelve Months

TYPICAL SPEECH AND
LANGUAGE DEVELOPMENT

Around your baby's sixth month or a little earlier, you will hear him repeating syllables. He will make a sound consisting of a consonant followed by a vowel and repeat it over and over. It may sound like "ba, ba, ba, ba," or "me, me, me, me." This is called **babbling** (see Glossary). Babies seem to enjoy both feeling and listening to what happens when they say these sounds over and over. This is useful. They need to associate the sound they make with the good feeling that goes with it. This helps them remember how to make it again. Babbling gives them this practice.

Babbling changes when your baby is around eight months old. He will say more syllables, and will say them in different ways. He may sound as if he's making a statement, giving a command, or asking a question. This change is important because it means that he is close to saying his **first meaningful word** (see Glossary). Not only is he "talking" more, but he is understanding more. Your eight-month-old baby will understand what you say by *how* you say it. He will react by being interested, happy, or frightened.

Don't be puzzled if your baby loses interest in babbling or imitating for a while. He is probably getting ready to learn something else—perhaps crawling, standing, or walking. He needs time to learn these things, too. When he's ready, you will find he will return to babbling again.

Up to now, you have been imitating your baby's "comfort sounds." Now is a time for you and your baby to begin to imitate each other. Imitate his babbling, smiles, scowls, hand-clapping, spoon-pounding, and throwing things (by tossing them back to him). When he babbles something to you, you should "babble" the same thing back to him. If you say something like "ma, ma," and he repeats it, then

you can consider this another sign that he is getting closer to saying his first meaningful word.

Your tone of voice is very important, for that is

how you show feelings. Be sure to speak slowly and let your voice, at times, show pleased excitement as well as disapproval. "Look what you did!" can be excited and happy when he takes his first steps. It can mean something altogether different when you discover he has thrown every single one of his toys out of his playpen.

Your baby understands words and phrases long before he can say them. He will respond to some words with gestures to show his understanding. For example, he may clap his hands when he hears you say "Pat-a-cake."

Don't be surprised if at around eight or nine months of age your baby suddenly becomes afraid of other people, even loving and familiar ones such as grandparents. This behavior is typical and healthy. He may feel anxious and worried that you are going to leave him. His fear of other people only means he is becoming more aware of differences, and the development of his feelings is continuing at a typical pace.

Around his first birthday, he should be able to follow one simple direction at a time. Such a direction might be "Come here," "Get down," or "Open your mouth." He should now be more aware that sounds make up words. He will gradually associate the words you say with the object, feeling, or activity they represent.

Children usually say their first meaningful word somewhere between nine months and a year and a half. When your baby uses a word with its true meaning, be sure to show your enthusiasm. Make him feel extremely proud of saying his first words. A smile and a hug will show him how pleased you are. He has no way of knowing just how important talking is. If you really show your happiness and excitement over these first words, he will want to say still more because it means so much to you—and he likes those hugs and smiles. Most grandparents and first-time parents find this easy to do!

When your baby begins to use meaningful words, it is time for you to *stop* imitating exactly what he says. Use the standard words instead. For instance, if your baby says "Aw gaw!" you should not repeat what he says; say "All gone!" instead.

When your baby says one of his first few words, remember he may be expressing the idea of a whole sentence. If he says "Go," he may mean "Where did Daddy go?" or "I want to go out." His first words will normally be one-word puzzles for you to figure out. He is sure to be puzzled by the words you use, too. It will help him understand you if you combine gestures and words. The words "Up we go!" or "Pat-a-cake" or "So big!" will mean more to him when they are put together with the right gestures. This is another step in developing the imitation skills that we will talk more about in later chapters.

A few words of caution: Don't make rules for your baby to follow at this age. Don't expect him to understand why you don't want him to do certain things. Babies react to angry words or punishment, but they don't *understand* why this is happening. Now is not the time to be concerned with making your child obey you. It is the time for you to do things your way without a big fuss, without spanking, scolding, or yelling. If he is "into everything," and likely to break or damage things that are important to you, remove them for now. Later, when he can understand that he might get hurt or damage something that is yours, then you can "discipline" him. This still doesn't mean you have to spank him or yell at him. There are other more effective ways of teaching him to obey you, and we will talk about these in a later chapter.

Another important thing your baby is *not* ready for at this age is toilet training. You will find this much easier to accomplish if you will wait until he is about two years old and he can tell you about his needs. For clues on how to tell when your child is ready for toilet training, see page 105.

Your baby is coming to know still more about you and about himself. Most of what he is learning is still being expressed and communicated through feelings. Now he takes up more of your time, because he is generally more active, and probably creeping and crawling. You and he are doing more things together as he progresses toward walking and talking. His muscle development, along with his listening and seeing skills, help him learn how he feels about himself and everyone around him. Sooner than you think, he will be able to put those feelings into words, and his words will reflect what he has learned from you. By imitating each other, first with comfort sounds, then babbling, then voice inflections, then body movements (such as smiles, frowns, and hand-clapping), you are getting him ready to talk and learn. By interacting with you, he is learning to feel good about himself. His first year is coming to a close. It is his first "getting ready" year, the first of many more to come. He is nearly ready to walk, talk, and learn much more from everyone around him.

In the beginning, your baby depended completely on you, his parents. Now he is ready to be shared with brothers, sisters, grandparents, aunts, uncles, and friends. Physically, he has grown tremendously, but he has also developed in other ways. You may ask yourself many questions about your baby's growth and development, but the most important question to ask yourself is this: How does he feel about you and about himself? No matter what other problems he may have, he is off to a great start if he likes being with you and you really like being with him. If you and your baby have been able to feel good as you talk, listen, see, and play together, good learning is happening. Doing things this way is not meant to make him learn more quickly. But it is an important way to prevent the development of difficulties we parents sometimes put in our child's path—difficulties that might cause problems later in life.

QUESTIONS ON DEVELOPMENT

Answer the questions in this section. If you can answer "yes" to at least half of them, your child is probably developing typically. If you cannot, then answer the questions for the next youngest age group. Keep working back until you can answer "yes" to more than half the questions in a section. This will give you an *approximate* age level of development for your child.

SIX TO NINE MONTHS: General

1. Does he change objects (such as a toy) from one hand to the other?

2. Does he sit by himself without support, or sit by leaning on his hands?

3. Does he sometimes sound as if he's trying to carry on a conversation with you?

4. Does he understand familiar words like "Bye-bye" and "Up we go" when they are used with gestures?

5. Does he recognize his name and a few familiar words?

6. Does he use any words that you recognize as if he really knew their meaning? Some common words you might hear him say are "Mama," "Dada," "me," "no," or "mine." He may even say the names of brothers, sisters, or family pets.

7. Does he stop what he's doing when you say "No, no"?

8. Does he recognize his mother by sight?

9. Does he wave bye-bye at the right time and understand games like "Pat-a-cake"?

10. Does he examine things carefully?

11. Does he grab or pull at objects and toys?

12. Is he suddenly afraid of other people?

NINE TO TWELVE MONTHS: General

1. Does he crawl on his hands and knees?

2. Does he sit unsupported for long periods of time while he plays with objects and toys?

3. Does he try to help when you dress him—for example, by pushing his arm into a sleeve?

4. Can he pull himself to a standing position?

5. Does he try to imitate facial expressions?

6. Does he try to imitate some of your gestures?

7. Does he use his voice to get attention?
8. Is he becoming friendlier to people?

9. Can he use two words or phrases (besides "Mama" or "Dada") that go with an action or object? Such words might be "Bye-bye," "Aw gone" (for "All gone"), "Nye-nye" (for "Nighty-night"), or "kah-kuh" (for "cracker").
10. Does he often wave and say "Bye-bye"?
11. If you laugh at something he's done, does he do it again?
12. Does he seem to enjoy listening to people talk?
13. Does he try to follow simple directions such as "Stand up," "Close the door," "Turn around," or "Come here" if you give them one at a time?

Physical Skills

1. Can he walk by holding on to things or when holding your hand?
2. Can he stand alone?

3. Can he drink from a glass or cup, if you help him hold it?
4. Can he put rings on a peg one after the other?
5. Can he roll a ball, imitating you?
6. Can he creep up stairs?
7. Does he put two or three blocks into a cup or other container?
8. Can he hold two things in one hand?
9. Will he play by himself for 10 to 15 minutes?
10. Does he like to feel his toys?
11. Does he like to be cuddled?
12. Is he beginning to use a spoon to feed himself?

After answering these questions, you may feel anxious; a lot of parents do. Just remember that *these questions on development represent averages only. Each child is different, and there will be many variations within the limits of what is typical.*

At this age, it is still rather early to try to figure out a child's level of development. If you are in doubt, remember the advice given in the chapter before this one. Go to your pediatrician, your local department of health, a mental-health center, or a well-baby clinic. You may also find help through United Way information services, a specialist in child development, your local schools, or a good nursery or day-care center. If you have questions, it will not hurt to seek advice, for your own peace of mind and for your child's well-being.

SUGGESTED ACTIVITIES

Time to Practice by Himself. Remember that it isn't necessary to spend every minute with your baby, for his sake as well as yours. He needs "alone time" to practice making sounds. When you hear him talking after he wakes up or when he's playing by himself, don't always interrupt. Sometimes just leave him alone. He needs to spend some time by himself as well as time with other people.

Talking to Him. Try to use short words and phrases when you're talking to your baby at this age. Use gestures with your words to help him understand what you mean. For example, wave your hand as you say "Bye-bye." Hold out your hands and say "Come" as you pick him up. Shake your finger when you say "No, no." As he begins to talk and use words with real meaning, use words that will be useful to him as you talk to him. Such words might be "Mama," "Daddy," "Let's go bye-bye," "Up!" or "Up we go!", and "Open your mouth." Say things like "Here's your *nose,*" emphasizing the word you want him to understand. Saying it two or three times will be helpful. Try to help him know the words that stand for things he can easily see, feel, or use. But don't expect your six-to-twelve-month-old baby to repeat after you every word you want him to learn. And *don't expect him to talk just as you do.* After all, he's only getting started. Give him time to say something, but don't pressure him to do so. Wait several seconds for him to "talk," and make sure you repeat the same thing several times. Don't change subjects too quickly or too often. A baby this age needs time to concentrate on one thing at a time, and it may take him quite a while to understand what you mean and get going on his own.

Listening. It is natural for children to be "hard of listening." Keep helping your baby learn to listen. Playing music for him is one way to begin. Hold your baby and dance or sway to the rhythm of the music. Clap your hands or his hands to the time of the music. He'll enjoy it even at this early age, especially if you sing or hum to him.

Call your baby's attention to all kinds of sounds. Talk to him about the sounds around the house—the doorbell, telephone, vacuum cleaner, or electric mixer. This will help him associate sounds and objects. Get him to talk about and imitate sounds. Try imitating some of the sounds you hear, like water running, the teakettle whistling, the alarm going off, or a door banging. Some of his toys may make noises, and you can imitate them, too. Get him to notice and imitate outdoor sounds—passing cars and trucks, honking horns, sirens, bells, dogs barking. If you live in the country, call his attention to the sounds made by birds or farm animals. Do all that you can with sounds, indoors and outdoors, to get your baby to listen to them and know what they are.

Playing with Things. Encourage your baby to play with toys that feel different and are of different shapes, sizes, and colors—but not with too many at one time. He can play with squeeze toys, soft dolls or stuffed animals, blocks, and balls. Look around your house for objects such as aluminum pie tins, small gift boxes, cereal boxes, tin cans with smooth edges, coffee cans with plastic lids, as well as those items already suggested for babies under six months. The kitchen is one of the best rooms in your home for finding things that will help your baby learn. Don't be in a hurry to toss out empty boxes and containers. With very little work, you can turn them into toys that will *let learning happen*.

(By the way, there is something you should know about and be prepared for. Some time between the ages of six and nine months your baby may be learning how to let go of objects. So expect him to throw everything out of his crib or playpen—and at mealtimes expect him to drop his spoon or a toy on the floor many, many times.)

All your baby's playthings should be objects he can safely chew on. Remember, too, that your baby will put just about everything he touches into his mouth, so keep out of his reach all toys and objects that are small enough for him to swallow. Give him things he can pick up, hold on to, turn over, and then drop. This will help him learn about things that are alike and things that are different. It will also give you many things to talk to him about. Name and talk about the things he is playing with, whether they are on the floor, in his crib, or in his bathtub. Make sounds that go with the things he is playing with. Imitate a toy car, train, or rubber duck. Make bubbling or splashing sounds as he has his bath. This lets him know there are sounds that go with things as well as sounds that go with doing things. Even as simple an activity as rolling over or being lifted high in the air should be talked about as it happens.

Give your baby something he can take apart and put together, like a small coffeepot. While he is playing with this, take a few minutes to talk to him about what he is doing. Say things like "Put it on," "On it goes," or "Off comes the top." (Don't use the words "lid" or "cover"; they are too hard for him to say.) Remember, learning by touching different things is very important. Learning by touching and hearing about what he is touching will help him get ready to learn to read. It will also give you things to talk to your baby about.

Crawling. When your baby begins to crawl around the house, be sure to keep out of his reach anything that might possibly hurt him. Put away or move out of reach anything you don't want him to touch, such as books and magazines, ashtrays, knickknacks, and plants. When he is a little older, he will understand that not everything in the house belongs to him and that he is not allowed to do anything he wants to. But for the time being, for his safety and your peace of mind, don't give him too many chances to get into trouble. Later on, you can turn the living room back into a living room, and everyone will breathe a little easier.

Now that you've taken these safety measures, don't keep your baby in a playpen or crib all day or even most of the day. Move the furniture around or use an expandable gate to make your living space into a giant play area. Allow your baby the freedom to explore and discover the world around him. This way, you can *let learning happen*. It's also good for his muscle development.

Imitation Games. You will notice that at this age your baby is becoming more interested in imitating you. For example, he may enjoy imitating your tongue movements, rolling a ball back and forth, clapping hands, or playing "peekaboo." Try all of these and see if he shows interest in imitating you.

PEEK A BOO!

Use the games below. If you use your imagination, perhaps you can change or add to them.

Have your baby point to his toes as you point to them, one by one, and say:
> This little pig went to market,
> This little pig stayed home,
> This little pig had roast beef,
> This little pig had none,
> This little pig cried, "Wee, wee, wee,
>   wee!" all the way home.

Encourage him to imitate the hand-clapping and "pat-a-caking" as you clap hands and say:
> Pat-a-cake, pat-a-cake, baker's man,
> Bake me a cake as fast as you can.
> Pat it and prick it and mark it with "B"
> And put it in the oven for baby and me.

Say, "How big are you?" and then help him answer by saying "So-o-o-o-o big!" as you raise his hands above his head. He should learn that when you say "How big are you?" he's to raise his hands above his head.
> "How big are you?"
> "So-o-o-o-o big!"

Say "Ah" as you slowly bring him to your face, and then gently say "Boo!" He'll learn to anticipate the "Boo" and eventually say it himself.
> "Ah-h-h-h-h-h . . . BOO!"

A baby this age will use repeated syllables and many voice gestures. Before he begins using meaningful words, be sure to copy what he says just as he says it. After he begins using meaningful words, make sure you always say these words in a grown-up manner, so he will learn to say them that way, too. Don't forget to imitate the tone and mood of his talking. This is part of his learning to listen.

Stacking Toys. You can buy stacking toys with plastic rings or wooden circles that can be stacked on a peg. Or you can make your own stacking toys with different-sized empty cans or containers. (Make sure there aren't any sharp edges.) Cooking pans or cardboard boxes also work. Stacking things helps develop hand-eye coordination, but it does much more than that. It gives you things to talk about: sizes (small, big, biggest); top and bottom (you can add middle later; it's a tough word for now); things that fall *down;* building something *up*. When you do this with him on your lap or close to you, you continue to build good feelings between the two of you, and good feelings within him about "belonging" and about himself.

Reading. Learning to read doesn't start in kindergarten or first grade. It starts now. Hold your baby on your lap as you look at a book or magazine together. This will be fun for both of you as you share the good feeling of doing something together. It will also make books and reading very interesting to your child. Let your child have a cloth book of his own— one that he can really scrunch up and chew on. This will let him know that books are things you really can have fun with. His first book should have only one picture on each page. He may not be interested in it for longer than two minutes at a time. That's fine. Don't force him to pay attention. Two minutes of paying attention and listening are worth ten minutes of squirming impatiently and not listening.

Mirror. When a baby begins to creep and crawl, he usually makes fewer sounds. This is because he's busy concentrating on these new skills. Since babbling is an important step in learning to talk, here is a way to encourage him to do more of it. Try putting a mirror near the floor so he can see himself in it. Play "peekaboo" in front of it, or just show an interest in him when he's there. Soon he will talk to himself when he is in front of it all alone.

Your Baby's Name. Begin to teach your baby his name by saying it often to him. Use the name you want him to be called when he grows up. Of course, you don't have to use your child's full name as it appears on his birth certificate. Most of us like to be called by an affectionate or shortened name like Andy or Jeanie or Bob. But don't call him "Junior" unless you want him to be "Junior" when he's 39. It is often difficult to drop nicknames. Being called by one's own name, not a childish nickname like "Sweetie" or "Honey," is part of building a good picture of oneself as a person. "Honey" may sound cute at age one or two, but it will be embarrassing at an older age.

Learning to See, Hear, and Touch. As a baby plays with his toes, hands, or toys, he is becoming aware that some things are alike and some are different. He learns that things are big or small, soft or hard, red or blue. As he looks at things, explain about them as you talk to him, but keep your explanations simple. Tell him only what he needs to know. If you supply the words that fit what he is seeing, hearing, or touching, you are helping learning happen and getting him ready for still more.

Your Baby's First Words. Your baby will probably say his first meaningful words somewhere between nine and eighteen months. He may say, "Bye-bye," "No, no," "Mama," "Hi," "mine," or "go." To encourage him, keep using the same words over and over. Be sure you give him time to say something to you. Remember to add a gesture whenever possible. But even though you should use gestures when talking to your baby, be careful *not* to respond only to his gestures. Don't teach him that grunting and pointing will get him what he wants. He has no way of know-ing if talking is worth all this trouble. If you show him that he can get what he wants an easier way, like pointing and grunting, or screaming and pointing, then that may be the way he will use.

Once he starts to talk, *never, never* criticize or correct the way he talks. If he doesn't say a word right, simply say it right for him and let it go. For instance, if he says "wah-wah" for water, give him water and say something like "Here's Billy's water." Emphasize the word *water,* saying it slowly and care-fully, but *don't* say "Now say it like Mommy," or "Say it like Daddy," or "Say it right," or "Say it over." That would be correcting and criticizing. Right now, he can't say it any better, but he did try. He did say something like the right word, and, most importantly, you were pleased and it got him what he wanted. Remember, do not correct or criticize—just continue to say words as you want him to say them. In time, he will imitate you.

Feelings. In all of the activities you and your baby share, feelings are very important. Whatever you do, you cannot separate feelings out and set aside time to work on them, any more than you can with his see-ing, hearing, or touching skills. They are all develop-ing at the same time, but sometimes we forget about feelings. I hope you have shared your *good* feelings, because your child will respond to your good feelings with good feelings of his own. Of course he will have other, not-so-good feelings, too. They may come from being hungry or tired, from having messy dia-pers, from being sick, or even from being allergic to certain foods or other things. Don't take feelings for granted. If you think about his feelings now, when he cannot talk, it will be easier for him to talk about them when he can.

Child Management. If he is "getting into everything," why not try these things:

1. Remove him without a lot of fuss.

2. Join him in an activity that will distract him and replace what he was doing.

3. Talk about how he might get hurt as you remove him from a dangerous scene. For instance, if he is near the stove, use the word "hot" in a tone that is not scolding but shows concern. This lets him know he has limits. Also, try using a concerned kind of tone and action, rather than a scolding tone, if he is likely to break a plant or a knickknack.

Setting schedules is important in helping you develop your managing skills. There aren't really too many to work with right now. However, eating and sleeping schedules are two of the most important ones that will help him get started.

If he won't eat at mealtimes, don't try to force him to eat, but don't let him snack between meals later on. He may be hungry before his next scheduled mealtime rolls around, but you can be sure he will not miss more than one meal if you stick to your guns. Remember, developing eating schedules that suit *both* of you is important.

If your baby frets and fusses and doesn't want to go right off to sleep at nap time or bedtime, you may be tempted to pick him up and bring him out into another room to quiet him down—or even to play with him. If you do, it won't take him long to realize that he can get you to do this whenever he wants, and you soon might find you have started a new sleeping routine. But don't ignore him completely if at times he cries harder. He may have a tummy ache or want some water or a pacifier. Attend to him quickly and gently. Just hold back on a lot of comforting sounds or touching. Calm him down as quickly and quietly as you can. This lets him know you are there but that he also has to go to sleep.

Remember, try to be consistent in order to help him learn what his schedules are. He knows nothing about limits or what is meant by being good or naughty. If you follow these guides, then he is learning about limits and schedules that are good for the whole family.

Remember, too, that you don't need to spend all your time with your baby. You are probably much too busy even to think of that. But if the short times spent together throughout the day are well spent, you will be giving him all he needs—your company, your love, and time to learn.

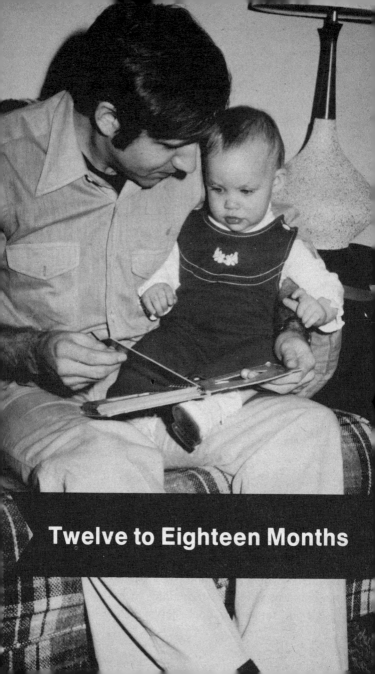

Twelve to Eighteen Months

TYPICAL SPEECH AND
LANGUAGE DEVELOPMENT

When your baby begins to walk, he will be exploring a whole new world. Learning through hearing, seeing, and touching will continue to happen all at once, even more than before. He'll discover that his legs (shaky as they may be) will carry him where he wants to go. When he begins to stand and move around, he will see things he has never seen before. He will be eager to investigate and to learn names for everything. The development of his muscles, large and small, and their coordination with what he sees and hears will begin to improve each day he explores his brand-new world. Many things will now be at his eye level—table tops, bookshelves, television knobs.

He may stand eye-to-eye with the family dog, or may even tower over a cat or smaller dog. All this is very new and exciting.

He will be seeing many more things, and handling them, if you let him. It's important for you to tell him the words that go with his new discoveries. Talk about the shape, size, color, feel, taste, and sound of just about everything. This is all part of developing his thinking processes. Right now, he is just beginning to use words. But by the age of five, children can use all sorts of words in many different ways. They use and know the differences between words like ''big,'' ''small,'' ''littlest,'' and ''tiny''; ''many,'' ''more,'' and ''none''; ''yesterday,'' ''today,'' and ''tomorrow.'' They can tell you all about animals that can hurt or animals that are fun. They know when something is upside down or inside out.

They can often do very special things such as spelling their own name and saying the alphabet. They can do all this, and more. But that all had to start somewhere, and it did—in the first year of life. Now, in his second year, your child is going to learn still more. Let's go back to his speech and language.

Although he probably says a few meaningful words, he needs your help to learn more. Give him a new word, or a short phrase that fits, every time he has a new experience. This may be, for instance, the first time he gets the hiccups. It may be when he

discovers a new object (such as the toilet bowl). Or it may be when he is puzzled about something (such as how a toy works). Saying simple words or phrases at the time your child needs them will help him understand what's going on (see **self-talk** and **parallel talk** in the Glossary).

He may need to hear words said again and again over a period of time before he tries to imitate them. This is typical and should be expected. Children learn to understand words before they use them meaningfully. You will probably grow tired of repeating the words long before he gets tired of listening, but he needs to keep hearing them.

As your child nears eighteen months, he should be able to say the names of several common objects. He won't be perfect, but he'll be close. He might say "baw" for ball, "poon" for spoon, and "tup" for cup. He may suddenly begin to repeat, too, many of the things you say. This is *not* a sign that he doesn't need any more help from you in learning to talk. Playing with imitation is a typical stage of speech and language development that happens at this time. Such parrotlike imitation is fine for giving your child

practice in making speech sounds, but it will teach him very little about what the words mean or how to use them.

There will be many times you won't like the way your child behaves. When he is about a year old, he is likely to scream, shake his crib, or do anything else he can to get your attention. He's not trying to be

naughty. He just doesn't have any other way to tell you how he feels. He may get very upset, and hit or bite you. Later, he may say things like "bad Mama" or "I hate you." You will probably hear him use expressions of anger that you have used. Let him know that it is all right to feel angry and say things like that. Remember, there will be times when he won't be able to do whatever he wants to do because you are busy or it just isn't safe for him. You can bet he will be angry or upset. Giving him words to express his emotions and then letting him use them is better than having him scream, cry, or throw things. In fact, it is better for both of you to get rid of feelings of anger rather than keep them bottled up. Give him the words he needs to show anger and sadness as well as happiness. When you express your anger, do it in a way that you would consider acceptable for him, too. Remember, if you're a door-slammer, wall-kicker, or nose-puncher, he's likely to become one too.

Children often test their parents to see how they will react. Your child might think "Did Mommy really mean it when she said not to take the pans out of the cupboard?" If you always respond in the same way when he tests you, he'll learn what he can do and what he cannot get away with. If he unrolls the toilet paper and you talk to him about it one time but ignore him the next, he'll really be confused. You have to teach him what you expect of him by *being consistent*.

Just a word about toilet training. By eighteen months, your child will be nearer to that time when you can most easily toilet train him. If you use the clues given on page 105 as your guide, you will know if he is ready to give it a try. Be patient and try *not* to hurry this activity. It will be easier on both of you and better for him if you wait until he is a little older.

QUESTIONS ON DEVELOPMENT

Answer the questions in this section. If you can answer "yes" to at least half of them, your child is probably developing typically. If you cannot, then answer the questions for the next youngest age group. Keep working back until you can answer "yes" to more than half the questions in a section. This will give you an *approximate* age level of development for your child.

TWELVE TO EIGHTEEN MONTHS: General
1. Can he say four to six different words?
2. Can he tell you what he wants by pointing and saying a few words?
3. Can he understand words and phrases when gestures are used?
4. Does he understand "Give that to me!" when it's used with appropriate gestures?
5. Can he help turn the pages of a book?
6. Can he walk alone?

7. Can he climb stairs on all fours without help?
8. Does he recognize the names of most common objects found in your home? Try out these questions, putting the words listed below in one or another of the blanks, one after the other.

    Where is the ____? Show me the ____. Give me the ____.

ball	scissors	bottle	window
table	cat	light	doll
bed	dog	diaper	toy car
door	stove	toy truck	apple

9. Does he point to the correct body parts when you say things like:

    Where is your mouth?   Where is your foot?
    Where is your eye?   Where is your leg?
    Where is your arm?   Where are your fingers?
    Where is your hand?   Where are your toes?

10. Does he use the names of familiar things, such as book, cup, spoon, water, or ball?

11. Does he seem to use the word "no" a great deal?
12. Does he say "Hi" and "Bye-bye" (or words that mean the same thing) at the right time?
13. Does he sometimes imitate the words you say in a parrotlike manner?
14. Does he like to listen to repeated rhymes, songs, and interesting sounds?
15. Can he eat with a spoon?
16. Can he stack three blocks?
17. Will he take four to five blocks from a box?

Physical Skills

1. Does he try to catch and throw a ball?

2. Does he turn the pages in a book, even though he usually turns more than one page at a time?
3. Does he pull a toy as he walks backward?
4. Does he climb into an adult-size chair?

5. Does he feed himself, even though he spills?
6. Does he walk upstairs holding on to an adult's hand?
7. Does he walk well enough so that he seldom falls?

After answering these questions, you may feel anxious; a lot of parents do. Just remember that *these questions on development represent averages only. Each child is different, and there will be many variations within the limits of what is typical.*

If, according to the "Questions on Development," your child's development seems to be a year or more behind his actual age, he may need some special attention. Talk to your pediatrician or a school psychologist if you have questions. You can also go to the well-baby clinic of a hospital or your local department of health. You may also find help through United Way information services, a specialist in child development, or a good nursery or day-care center.

SUGGESTED ACTIVITIES

Being a Good Teacher. You have worked very hard at developing your child's imitation skills and forming a good emotional relationship between you and your child. Now, in his second year of his life, these will have a great influence on his learning to talk. You are the model for your child's speech and language, so it's important that you speak slowly, clearly, and simply. If you want to understand how hard it is for him to learn to talk, imagine yourself in a foreign country listening to a foreign language. You would try first of all to understand the meaning of all those strange sounds. The foreigner to whom you're listening could help if he would use as few words as possible, and be sure to add plenty of gestures. Also, if he pronounced his words clearly and slowly, you would have an easier time learning to repeat them. If the person you were talking with pointed to whatever he was talking about, it would help you understand even faster. If you were trying to learn the words, you would need to hear them many times before you would feel comfortable about using them. With this in mind, try to remember these important rules:

1. Use simple, clear, slow speech when talking to your child.
2. When you are going to do something new, talk about what you're going to do before you do it, while you're doing it, and after it's all over.
3. Start with words that are useful—foods, body parts, clothing, toys, family names.
4. Make your child feel that he is part of what is going on, not just an observer.

5. Talk *with* him. Give him a chance to add his two cents worth—even if you can't understand it. Listen to what he says. Make him feel that what he says is definitely important.

6. When using new words, make sure he can see the way you're saying them, as well as being able to hear them.

7. *Do not expect or demand perfection.*

Self-Talk. When your child is nearby, talk out loud about what *you* are hearing, seeing, doing, or feeling.

DISH...WASH THE DISH WITH WATER

Let him know there are words to describe all sorts of activities and feelings. For example, as you are hanging up clothes, dusting the furniture, making the beds, washing the car, or setting the table, talk about the things you are doing. Be sure to talk slowly and clearly, and to use simple words and short phrases. "Romper Room" and "Captain Kangaroo" are television programs that use this kind of self-talk. Watch them to see how it is done. (You may have to find reruns of these programs.)

Parallel Talk. Parallel talk is different from self-talk. In parallel talk, you talk about what is happening to your child. Use words that describe what *he* is doing, seeing, hearing, or feeling. This gives him words to think with. He will use them later when he wants to tell you about things that are happening to him.

"BILLIE IS CLIMBING UP CLIMBING RIGHT UP"

Listening. Learning to listen is still important, so keep working on it. Your child needs help in understanding all that he is hearing. Outdoors, try to make him notice noises of engines running, trucks braking, dogs barking, leaves rustling, birds singing, the wind blowing. Inside the house, you and he will hear doors closing, water running, someone walking, a mixer in the kitchen, the furnace starting, the clock ticking, the vacuum cleaner running, or the teakettle whistling. You may have already called your child's attention to some of these sounds. That's okay. They are still good sounds to listen to and talk about.

Talk about those sounds and any others you think of, especially if he asks about special sounds his toys make. Many activities will also help build listening skills. Here are a few of them:

1. Give your child simple directions like "Bring me the ball." Each time, make it a different object, something that is familiar to him. He will be eager to show that he understands you. Make sure he knows you're proud of what he is doing, and be sure to use parallel talk.

2. Try the tune "Here we go 'round the mulberry bush," adding your own lines such as "This is the way we wash our hands, wash our hands, wash our hands. This is the way we wash our hands, so early in the morning." Other short phrases, like "eat our soup," "comb our hair," "brush our teeth," can also be used. Show him how to act out each new line. It helps build his imitation skills and it's fun.

3. Play "follow-the-leader." This is especially good with other children in the family. They can line up and the leader can give directions like "Pat your head," "Clap your hands," or "Go behind the chair." Even a one-year-old child can play this.

4. Encourage him to play "Ring around the rosy." This is a good listening game. If there are older

children, they can help teach the younger ones.

5. "Hide and seek" is a game that little children usually enjoy. Don't make it too hard. Call to him from your hiding place if he takes too long to find you, or let a little of you show until he gets good at it. This is another good time to use parallel talk as he tries to find the people who are hiding.

6. Let him listen to people on the telephone. Let him say a few words to them. Children this age are curious about voices on the telephone, but they say very little themselves until they become more familiar with it.

7. Television programs like "Captain Kangaroo," "Sesame Street," and "Romper Room" provide good listening experiences for children of this age. Watch these shows with your child and try some of the same kinds of activities.

8. When swinging a child this age, remember to stand in front of the swing to push him. It will be less scary and more reassuring, and he can see you as you say things like "Up you go!" and "Down you come!" Give him as many opportunities as possible to hear you use short, simple, clear words and phrases.

9. There are records that will help your youngster listen to sound differences and encourage imitation. These are mentioned in a listing of "Records for Children" on page 241.

Child Management. Your child needs time to be alone, to help him become independent. It's possible he may get to depend on you too much. You will have to work at helping him overcome this. There may be times when you are too busy to play with him, and he must get used to that. To make this easier, take time out for short periods during the day to play with him, sometimes for as little as two or three minutes. He will usually be contented with that, and then go on playing by himself. Don't always wait for him to call you. Just pop in on him. Other times, when he calls you, tell him you'll be there in a few minutes, a little while, or pretty soon. Then make sure you show up shortly. Don't forget about him and have him anxiously call you again. Sometimes it helps to make a little noise every now and then, just to let him know that you are around. Later on, if there are other children in your home, they can help by playing with him from time to time. Right now, however, it's his mother and father who count the most. He will be imitating you more than ever, so be a good model for him to follow. Becoming self-confident, acting independently, feeling good about yourself, and getting ready to face the world take a lot of doing at eighteen months, but they are possible with your help.

Touching. Let your child handle things that are different in shape, size, weight, and texture. This will give him practice at using his fingers to get ideas and information about his world. Make sure he has a chance to handle and touch all sorts of things, such as different kinds of cloth, as well as objects that are rough, smooth, heavy, furry, soft, round, square, big, or small. Talk to him about how they are different and how they are alike.

Making a Scrapbook. Collect large, brightly colored pictures of things your child is familiar with and whose names he can say or likes to try to say. Paste these in a scrapbook, adding a picture to the book for each word he can say. This will help him learn more words. Paste the pictures on pieces of cardboard. You can get this at a dime store, or you can cut up boxes you bring home when you go shopping. Make holes near the edge of the cardboard, and use small notebook rings or pieces of yarn to hold the pages together. Heavy pages last longer and are easier for a child to turn. A book like this gives you something to use when you help your child practice words he has learned. Always make looking at his book a fun thing to do. Expect that he won't say words the same way you say them, and remember, *don't correct him.* Just say each word the correct way.

Reading. Read books to your child. Good books for his age are those with simple, colorful pictures.

Look at the list "Books for Children" on page 233 for suggestions. Your child may enjoy looking at books alone, too. When you give him a book, be sure he knows it's *his* book. Give him books that are inexpensive enough so that if he tears the pages, no one will worry. An old trading-stamp catalog or mail-order catalog is really a good choice. Catalogs are designed to be attractive to both grown-ups and children. As you look at the pictures, you can choose just about anything you want to name, whether it's toys, food, or clothing. In each group or category you can talk about how things are different, and how they are alike.

Finger Plays. Show your child a few simple finger plays (see the section "Finger Plays" on page 225). Several of the plays listed there are suitable for this age. Choose at first those that have only a few words and only one or two finger movements, like "Jack-in-the-Box" or "Here's the Church."

New Words. When you explain a new word, it helps if you can use a word your child already knows. For instance, you might say a bird's *nest* is a bird's house; a *bus* is like a big car; a *lion* is like a big kitty. When you explain the differences, try to do so in short, simple, clear sentences.

Toys. Just giving your child toys, whether homemade or bought, isn't enough. You should spend some time showing him how to use them. More than ever, make sounds that go with the toys. Say "rrrr," imitating a siren, for a fire engine, and "quack, quack" for a duck. You don't have to spend a lot of time with your child. Just make sure that when you are playing together, you give him your time and attention, without two dozen interruptions in less than half an hour. The way you spend time together is more important than how much time you spend together.

Let your child decide what to do with his toys. Don't be like the father who started to help his son build with blocks but used most of them to finish his own giant castle! Try not to be bossy when showing him ways to use his toys. Let him play in his own way.

The following suggestions can be useful in several ways. They help develop muscle coordination, especially hand-eye coordination. Also, because they give you a chance to sit down for a few minutes with your child, they help to develop that good emotional feeling between the two of you. If you continue to do this, his self-confidence and good feelings about himself will continue to grow.

At Twelve Months:
1. *Giant Snap-Lock Rings and Beads*. These are pull-apart, snap-together rings and beads of assorted shapes. They come in bright colors and are made of washable plastic.
2. *Wooden or Plastic Blocks*. They are made in different colors, shapes, and sizes. You will find that at first your child will do very little organized playing or building with the blocks. Later on, he will probably stack or balance them and enjoy dumping them out of containers. Homemade blocks can be made by cutting off the tops of pint or half-pint milk cartons or cutting

wood into block-size pieces. (Be sure there are no rough parts that can cause splinters.)

3. *Ball Rolling*. Sit about four feet from your child and roll a large ball back and forth between you. He will probably be a little older before he will learn to throw a ball.

4. *Pull or Push Toys*. They have long handles or strings so that they can be pulled or pushed around. Some of the commercial ones make noise as they are moved. Unless you have insensitive ears or nerves of steel, it is best to find one that does not make much noise. On the other hand, the noise will help you know just where your child is. You can make your own pull toys. String some empty shoe boxes together with heavy string to make a train. Make sure the string is long enough in the front for pulling. Knot a string and run it through the center of a lid from a round oatmeal carton. Put a handful of

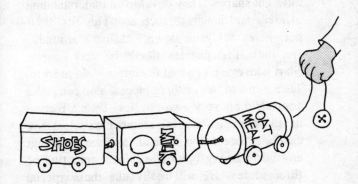

dry macaroni inside the box, then tape the lid back on. Put a button on the end of the string so he can pull it easily. Round ice cream containers can be used the same way.

At Eighteen Months: The next group of toys is especially good for children about eighteen months old.

1. *Bead Stringing.* Let him string large wooden beads on twine or string. Use empty thread spools to make a homemade set. Paint them if you like. Just make sure you use paint that contains no lead and is safe for children. Make a big knot at one end of the string or twine and tape the other end like a shoelace tip so he can string the spools easily.

2. *Fit-together Puzzles* (with one, two, or three pieces). It will be easier for your child if each piece has a framelike form to fit into. I want to say a special word about puzzles. They are good for so many things. They help hand-eye coordination. They sharpen a child's ability to "see" different shapes. They develop an understanding of ideas and language such as "This fits," "It goes here," "Upside down," "Turn it around." But these first puzzles should be very simple. Start with one piece that fits into a mold or form. Then move to two or three pieces. You can make your child his very own puzzles. Take a picture he likes from a trading-stamp catalog or toy catalog. Paste it on a piece of cardboard cut from any fairly heavy box. Then cut it into two or three pieces. He will really like these special puzzles because you made them for him.

It's really important for you to start your child with puzzles *now*. This will help him with many things he will be learning as he grows older.

3. *Objects for Crawling or Climbing.* Children this age like to crawl and climb, to get on top of, inside, and under all sorts of things.

   A. From an appliance store, get a large cardboard box in which a refrigerator or stove was shipped. Cut a door and window that will open and close to make an indoor playhouse. Your child will play in it for hours.

   B. Cut holes in opposite sides of cardboard cartons to make a tunnel. Don't cut a whole side of the carton out. You need the outer part of each cut side to support the "roof." Make the tunnel as long as you can.

C. Place a board across two closed books lying
flat on the floor. This will raise the board
slightly off the floor and make a bridge to
walk or crawl over.

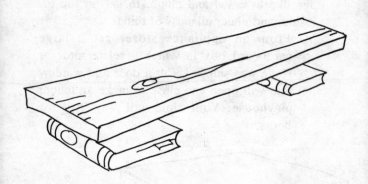

4. *Crayons*. Show your child how to use crayons.
Most children of this age seem to do better with
large, kindergarten-sized crayons, though some
may like the smaller ones. Large crayons don't
break as easily and are easier to hold. Tape paper
to the floor for him so he can really spread out.
Don't give him coloring books, and don't expect
him to make coloring-book types of pictures.
Even if you can't tell what he is drawing, show
him that you really like his creation.
5. *Sandbox*. A small plastic swimming pool holds
about the right amount of sand. A sandbox can
also be made by digging a shallow hole, then lin-
ing the sides and bottom with boards or a piece of
heavy plastic. This type can be made large
enough for as many children as needed.

Right-Handed or Left-Handed? If you are not sure which hand your child uses most or seems the most comfortable with, it is possible to help him decide without any pressure whatsoever. The first thing you want to do is find out which hand he does use or likes to use. As you give him things, don't reach toward either the right hand or the left hand. Instead, head for the middle of his body and see which hand he reaches out. When you set his place at the table or at his high chair, put his spoon at the top of his plate, in the middle. Watch to see which hand he uses to pick it up. When you play with him, either on the floor or at a table, put his toys in front of him. Again, watch to see which hand most often picks up the toys. If he is completely undecided or definitely *not* left-handed, then I suggest you help him become right-handed—but this should be done without any pressure whatsoever. Each time you give him something, direct the object toward the right hand. When you set the table for him, put his spoon and cup on the right side. When you dress him, start with the right side. Put his right arm in his undershirt or shirt first, then the left arm. Put his right pant-leg on first, then his left. Put his right sock and shoe on, then his left sock and shoe, and when he wears a coat or jacket, put his arm in the right sleeve first. Follow the same practice when you undress him.

If you know for sure your child is left-handed, I would not try to change it. However, it is better for him to be either right-handed or left-handed than to use both hands equally. Being definitely right-handed or definitely left-handed will help him later in developing his reading skills and general body coordination.

One last important word about right-handedness and left-handedness. After you are sure you have found out which hand your child uses more, then relax the constant attention to one side of his body. Occasionally, hand things to his left side, dress and undress him starting with the left side, and so on with other activities. While it is important for him to be definitely right-handed or left-handed, it is also essential for him to learn to use the opposite hand and foot. For example, being able to hop or stand on either foot is important in developing his muscle coordination.

Toilet Training. Don't start toilet training much before the age of two. Most children are not ready until after that second birthday. You will find it can be accomplished more quickly if you wait for these clues from your child:

1. He will have a bowel movement at a regular time.
2. He will stay dry most nights.
3. He will be able to hold urine for longer periods of time.
4. He will have enough understanding to know what is expected of him when he is on the potty or toilet seat.

Too much concern about toilet training, or scolding and shaming a child when he wets or soils his pants, will only create a stumbling block in a parent-child relationship. All too often, toilet training begins at the time that children are learning their first word. For a few children, this is fine. But for the typical child, the additional demands of toilet training are more than he can handle. Toilet training is a step in social development that depends not only on a child's physical ability to control himself, but also on his communication skills. If he can't understand what's expected of him, or tell you his needs, then he can't be expected to perform. Have patience. He's coming to that point where he will know what is expected and he will want to please you. He will be trying harder. Help him by words of encouragement after dry nights and when he shows an interest in using the bathroom.

Eighteen to Twenty-Four Months

TYPICAL SPEECH AND LANGUAGE DEVELOPMENT

This is a most exciting time for you and your child. It is hard to stop saying "baby" and start using the word "child." But now that his words are beginning to flow and he is really talking to you, he truly cannot be called a baby any more. Now he is about to become a big two-year-old, and he will be using so many more words that he will seem to go ahead by leaps and bounds. This alone will make him seem more "grown up," no longer a baby and well on his way to achieving excellent speech and language skills. However, he still has a long road ahead. He needs all the help he can get from you and the rest of the family.

Here is an important thing to remember: As your child says words and sentences, *never correct or criticize him!* Just repeat the word or phrase correctly, as you would want him to say it. For instance, if he says "Me milk want," simply say "I want milk. Here's your milk," as you hand him the milk. It will show that you understand and it tells him the right way to say it. You simply need to be a good model for him to copy.

An eighteen-month-old child will typically be able
to say ten or more words, but it is possible for him to
be using as many as 300 words by the time he is two

MOMMY DADDY
BROTHER SISTER
ME WATER MILK
WHAT'S THAT BABY
PLUG RADIO NO NO
TRUCK FIREMAN
DOGCATCHER BOO
INTERESTING SHOE
I WANT NO SOAP
SUPERDOOPER

COME LOOKY SEE
AH YES OH STAR
MOON FUN SUN
SKY TELEVISION
DOLLY BEDDYBYE
WON'T SLEEP GO
RIDICULOUS OOPS
NOW WOW OW
ASTRONAUT

years old. This is the time that most children begin to
put words together to make two-word sentences.
Help him learn new words, but don't expect him to
talk like an adult. Why? Because his memory span is
still limited. He needs to develop control of the muscles used to make difficult sounds as well as those
used to talk at a faster rate. He doesn't know enough
words to talk about all his ideas, and he must learn
more about putting words together to make up sentences.

Many children of this age will try to talk as fast as
their parents. This often results in a kind of jabber
that we call **jargon** (see Glossary). In contrast to
babbling, jargon is full of many different sounds, and

is both very expressive and quite meaningless. When a child uses jargon, he will be excited, talking faster than usual. He may have a lot of expression in his voice. Don't make fun of the way he is talking. Accept it as okay. Just don't interfere with him when you hear him use it. He will generally use jargon when he is talking to his toys or pets. Or, he may never use jargon; that is equally okay. If your child uses jargon, it will probably disappear by the time he is two-and-a-half years old.

Reading to your child continues to be important for many reasons. He will now be able to talk more about the stories, which helps him build sentences and language skills. You can point out smaller parts of a picture. This helps him learn by seeing. He will be rapidly adding many new words to those he knows. Besides, it's *always* nice for him to sit cuddled up next to you or on your lap.

You are going to wonder where all his energy is coming from. Some days keeping up with him will seem almost impossible. His muscle coordination needs help now, so plan games or little jobs around the house that will give him practice—things like picking up his toys, being his mother's or father's helper, or just chasing him around the table.

He is coming to that time when he will want to range far and wide to look the world over, and you may often wonder where he is. If you happen to leave the gate or front door open, or if he figures out how to unlock them, you may find him outside wearing nothing but a big grin. He seems to know no fear.

Setting limits will really be a task. He must begin to

learn more about dangerous places and things such as streets and cars. If you live on a farm, he must learn more about dangerous farm machines and animals. Be consistent with what you say and do when he starts to find out about these things. This will help him understand his limits. If you do not want him to leave the backyard or wander down the street without you, then stick to that rule very time he tries.

For all his growing independence, your child still wants and needs to be cuddled and be given plenty of support. Give him hugs, smiles, and little pats from the top of his head to his bottom. He will be exploring more with his hands, eyes, and ears and will seem to get into everything. This curiosity is good, even though some days it may drive you to distraction.

As he nears two years of age, your child will probably be ready for toilet training. If you waited for the clues mentioned on page 105, you will know if he is ready to learn. Mother or father can serve as a model for this learning, just as you have for other activities.

Your child will be inquisitive about what you are doing, your body parts, and the sounds he hears when you go to the bathroom or take a bath. Remember, he is learning many more words now, so this will be a good time to use the standard words for body parts and their functions when he asks about them. It is a good time to learn about natural, necessary human functions, and the names of the body parts used to perform these functions in a very natural way. Do not be concerned about privacy right

now. He will learn about this when he can understand what it means. Now he is becoming interested in what happens when you are in the bathroom and using the toilet or taking a bath. If you will be a model for your child to imitate, you will make his toilet training much easier to understand and learn. You can also teach him the standard words for body parts and uses in the same natural, easy way.

However, this may not be easy for all parents. Some people are more comfortable with nudity, and have a more open family approach in helping children learn about body parts and functions. But many of us have strong feelings of privacy in regard to these matters. If you are not comfortable having your child in the bathroom with you, don't try to fake it. Your child will sense your uneasiness if you try to do things and use words that do not come naturally to you. This will only make him confused and uneasy, too. So if you are uncomfortable about serving as a model for your child's toilet training or bathing, then don't do it.

This may also be the time that a little brother or sister joins the family. It will help your child understand and get ready for the changes that will take place if you begin to talk about the new baby's arrival. Whether the baby will arrive by birth or adoption makes no difference. Talk about it beforehand. Two-year-olds often do not notice a mother's gradual change in shape and size. If he does, however, that would be a good time to begin to talk about a new brother or sister. If he doesn't notice, then begin to talk about the new arrival (or a planned adoption) several weeks in advance of the event.

Remember that so far your first-born has had your complete attention, but now he must share you. After the new baby comes, plan as quickly as you can to spend some time alone regularly with your older child. This is more difficult if there is only one parent to be shared between children—but it is very important. A lot of changes take place when a new baby arrives, and it won't be easy for your first-born to understand them. You, as an adult, understand about such changes, and can cope with them. You knew long in advance that the new baby was coming, and were ready for it. But how can you help your older child adjust to the new arrival?

Don't be surprised if he seems to dislike or be jealous of the new baby. You can tell him that he doesn't have to love his new brother or sister, but that he *must not hurt* the baby. Remember, also, that an infant should not be left alone with a two- or three-year-old. Accidents sometimes "just happen." Little ones have to learn that littler ones need help and protection. Share the new baby with your older child as much as you can. You should also try to manage your schedules to give him "alone-time" with both his mother and his father. He knows that someone else is taking your time and attention. Learning to handle that is a step in adjusting to changing situations in his life.

QUESTIONS ON DEVELOPMENT

Answer the questions in this section. If you can answer "yes" to at least half of them, your child is probably developing typically. If you cannot, then answer the questions for the next youngest age group. Keep working back until you can answer "yes" to more than half the questions in a section.

This will give you an *approximate* age level of development for your child.

EIGHTEEN TO TWENTY-FOUR MONTHS:
General

1. Does he put together words that express two or more ideas, such as "Daddy go bye-bye"?
2. Does he know about twenty or more words that he uses in talking?
3. Does he often gesture when he talks?
4. Does he rely more on words and less on gestures to get his ideas and feelings across?
5. Has he begun to use words like "mine," "me," and "you"?
6. Does he enjoy games in which he names things he sees?
7. Does he try to use words to express his physical needs or to answer questions (but not necessarily to carry on a conversation)?
8. Does he frequently use two-word sentences?
9. Does he use words to ask for things or to describe the things going on around him?
10. Does he know his boundary limits—when you go shopping, when he plays outdoors, or when you go for a walk?
11. Does he help undress himself?
12. Can he match similar objects?
13. Does he enjoy listening to simple stories, especially those he's heard before?
14. Does he ask you to tell him the names of things with questions like "What's this?" or "What's that?"

15. Does he understand and follow single directions, like "Put the ball on the chair," "Sit down," "Turn around," "Bring me the paper," "Give the ball to me," or "Pick up the ball"?

16. Does he show you he understands by pointing to the appropriate picture when you ask "Show me a dog," "Show me a man," or "Show me a hat"?

Physical Skills

1. Can he turn the pages of a book one at a time?
2. Can he scribble with a pencil or crayon?
3. Can he draw something that is more or less circular in shape, if you first show him how?
4. Can he usually run without falling?
5. Does he build a tower of blocks five or six blocks high by himself?
6. Does he use a rocking chair with help?

After answering these questions, you may feel anxious; a lot of parents do. Just remember that *these questions on development represent averages only. Each child is different, and there will be many variations within the limits of what is typical.*

If, according to the "Questions on Development," your child's development is a year or more behind his actual age, he may need some special attention. Talk to your pediatrician or a school psychologist if you have questions. You can also go to the well-baby clinic of a hospital or the local health department to get answers to your questions. You may also get help through United Way information services, a specialist in child development, or a good nursery or day-care center.

SUGGESTED ACTIVITIES

Being a Good Teacher. Turn back to page 89 and review the description of how to be a good model for your child's speech and language.

Following Directions. Give your child practice in following directions. When you give him directions to follow, try to talk about things that are important to him and that he already knows about. Have him point out his own body parts, as you say "Where are your eyes?" "Where is your nose?" (or mouth, or hair, and so on). Be sure not to *demand* the answer. If he doesn't know, show him. Ask him to carry out two directions, like "Bring me your car and the bunny," or "Pick up your blanket and put it on the bed."

Reading. Choose colorful books with large, simple pictures. (See the list of books for children on page

233.) The library is a great place to get books that are just right for your child's age. You don't have to read a story exactly as it is written. Make up your own simple version, using short sentences. Point out the action in the pictures and the things you are talking about. Give him a chance, and he will eventually fill in some key words of the story. (But don't demand that he do this.) He may want you to read a favorite story over and over, even though you get tired of it.

Going Places and Doing Things. Your child is ready for new experiences. Help him get to know and understand the world he lives in. When you go places and do things, it will help him if you remember to talk about it before you go, talk about it while you're there, and then talk about it after you're home or when it's all over. Also remember to use *parallel talk* and *self-talk*.

You can start out with some of the following easy places to go or things to do:

Visit a park.

Talk about his TV program.

Have a backyard picnic.

Go to the airport.

Go to his grandparents' house.

Visit a museum.

Go to a carnival or circus.

Enjoy a family vacation or outing.

Attend special children's events.

Visit a farm or a town (depending
   on where you live).

Go for a walk.

Visit people.

Visit the zoo.

Go fishing.

Go out to eat.

Wash the car.

Go for a Sunday afternoon drive.

See special community events, such as
   a July 4th or Memorial Day parade.

Pictures on Cards. It's now nearly impossible to keep a scrapbook of *all* the new words your child is learning to say. But try to find pictures of some of them and paste them in a scrapbook. Or, for something different, paste them on 5″ × 8″ cards. He can show these picture cards to people, especially his grandparents, naming those he remembers and being helped with the others.

Records. There are children's records of good music, nursery rhymes, and stories that can open up whole new worlds of experience to him. Remember that the public library usually has records. You will find that many libraries offer them on loan without any charge whatsoever. (See the list "Records for Children" on page 241.)

Toy Telephones. Use toy telephones for conversations with your child or let him use a play phone to talk to other children. This helps build language skills, especially using longer sentences. Buy a toy telephone or make one youself. A play telephone can be made out of a milk carton, a shoebox, or any other

small box. Cut a round hole in the side of the box to hold the receiver. Make the receiver out of an empty toilet paper roll core (seal one end) and attach it to the box with yarn or string. Color or paste a picture of a telephone dial on the front of the box.

Talking Toys. There are several kinds of talking toys—dolls, stuffed animals, telephones, toy TV sets. Some are shaped like clocks with a pointer that points to pictures. These toys usually have a string that has to be pulled to make the toys work. Be sure a talking toy sounds clear and is easily understood before you buy one. Your child may find it interesting for a while. When he does, call his attention to the sounds it makes or the words it says. Show him how to make the toy work. Tell him what to listen for and repeat some of the sounds and words to remind him about imitation.

Pounding Bench or Peg Board. Hammering pegs will help your child work off a little steam, and will also give him a chance to feel he is accomplishing something. Doing simple tasks over and over is good for him. Pounding, for instance, uses up energy and also develops hand-eye control. It's a helper for developing muscle coordination. It can also make him feel good if you tell him many times what a big boy he is when he pounds in those pegs. You might even give him a real hammer with some large nails and let him pound them in an old board, if the wood is soft enough. Be sure you stay to help, and watch him very closely if you do let him use a real hammer and nails. A small tack hammer may be more his size.

Puzzles. A child this age should be able to play with three- or four-piece puzzles, especially if he has been doing simpler ones earlier. When he is working on a puzzle, use parallel talk. Teach the idea of something being "in," "on," "next," "over there," "beside," and "by the big one."

Ripping and Tearing. Before children learn to make things—and even afterward—they like to tear things. Let your child rip old magazines and newspapers. Show him how to tear and poke holes in paper. Use tissue paper, heavy construction paper, old gift-wrapping paper, grocery bags, old greeting cards. Ask him "Can you tear a little piece?" or "Can you tear a big piece?" Paste what he tears out on a large piece of paper. Talk about the feel of the different kinds of paper. As he makes things for you, be sure to put some of them up where all the world can see how he is doing. It doesn't matter if it's just something pasted together, or a few crayon scribbles on a piece of paper. Let him know you think he's great. This is just another step in building his self-confidence and good feelings about himself.

Water Time. "Water and children" is a natural combination, just like "bacon and eggs." There are

so many different ways to play with water. Splashing, pouring, tasting, spilling, drinking, dunking (teddy bears or food), mixing (with dirt or sand) are just some of the things you can do with water or other liquids. Let him do all of these things, but again, not alone. It's more fun—and safer—if you join in. This is an activity that's good for extending his attention span. Use plastic (not glass) containers for safety's sake. Use parallel talk and self-talk, depending upon who's doing the action.

Child Management. This is more than just saying "No, *no,* NO!" We suggest you count the number of times you say "no" to your child on an average day. You might be surprised! If you find that you are saying "no" to what he's doing most of the time, try one of these alternatives:

1. Say nothing. Just remove him from the situation.
2. Tell him that you don't like to see children doing

what he's doing and that you want him to stop. If he thinks he's made you unhappy, he may stop right there. But don't shout "Billy, I'm sick and tired of your teasing! Now get out of here! You've been bad all day! Wait 'til your Dad gets home! He'll fix you! No, no, no!" (Swat.) Instead, look directly at him and say something like this in as calm a voice as possible: "I don't like to see a boy pulling his sister's hair. It makes me mad when I see a big child pick on a little one. I get very upset when I see it. I want it stopped right now."

3. Set limits. The limit might be "You are not to pull your sister's hair." When he breaks the rule, ask him to tell you what the rule is. When children repeat a rule often enough, it seems to help prevent unwanted behavior.

4. Give him a choice. (This is the big step!) "Stop pulling her hair *or* you will be sent to your room." If he keeps on pulling her hair, then make sure that your threat of sending him to his room is carried out. Make *him* feel responsible for deciding to change his behavior. How can you do this? You might say something like "When you think you can stop fighting or pulling your sister's hair, you can come back into the room." He then has to make a decision! If he comes back and soon starts fighting or causing a fuss, again remove him immediately, saying something like "Well, I guess you really weren't ready to come back. You'll just have to think about it some more."

Now if I know two-year-olds, yours will probably go to Step Four quickly. There are several important things to remember. First, don't bargain. If he pulls his sister's hair one more time, after you have given him a choice, don't back out. Take him to his room. He has to learn that he has limits, and that he has just reached one. So, off he goes. If his room is full of toys and fun things to do, choose a room that isn't full of "goodies." Don't put him in a room where he can watch television. It really won't matter that he has been taken off somewhere to make him think about what he has done if he has a television or toys to play with. He won't have time to think. He will be too busy playing.

Make the length of time he spends alone in his room (or wherever you decide to put him) fit in with the seriousness of his actions. He should be kept there the longest time for doing something that is dangerous to himself or others, like running into the street. In general, keep his "away-from-the-fun" time short. It won't take him long to realize that you mean business.

Remember that starting now, and for many years to come, your child wants to please you. He wants your love and approval. If you let him know he has these, you will find that sharing in all his learning processes will be a wonderful and enjoyable thing.

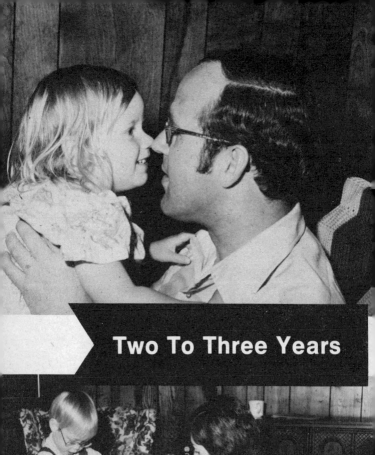

Two To Three Years

TYPICAL SPEECH AND LANGUAGE DEVELOPMENT

Will all your child's speech sounds be used correctly? No, they won't, so don't expect or demand perfection. If you do, you may set back much of the good emotional relationship you have developed between you and your child. You may also set back a good deal of his own self-confidence and good feelings about himself. Here is what you can expect for the next few years.

Children this age will change a sound or substitute one sound for another (like saying ''thun'' for ''sun''). They may also leave a sound out of a word altogether (like saying ''wing'' for ''swing''). Even though sound differences like these are typical for a two-year-old child, he should still be able to make all the vowel sounds and some of the consonant sounds. (See ''Speech Sounds'' on page 217 for a better understanding of the sounds that a child may be expected to make at different ages.)

One of the most important discoveries your child will make is that words are said with individual speech sounds put together in different ways. He will then begin to understand that words have a sound at the beginning, sounds in the middle, and a sound at the end. He will discover that part of learning to talk is understanding how to put sounds together to make words. At this age, your child may play with sounds by rhyming words or by changing the beginning or ending of familiar words. He may say "poo, pay, pee, pow" or "house-oh," "table-oh," "spoon-oh," "mommy-oh." As he does this, he is learning how words can be changed and having fun at the same time. But it is also practice that will eventually help him improve the way he says words.

His vocabulary should increase to about 900 words between his second and third birthdays. Don't try to count the words he knows. You'll know there are at least that many by the way he chatters and asks you question after question. A three-year-old should be able to tell you his thoughts and feelings in sentences of four or five words. He may even use longer sentences, because a child who is three will be using more words and have better control of the muscles used for speech.

How Can You Help Your Child Improve His Grammar?

Simplify your own way of speaking, so your child has a model that is easy to copy. Rephrase what your child has said if it is grammatically incorrect, but use similar words. After he says "Car no go," you say "The car won't go." If he is nearby, try some self-correction, such as "Me want coffee. No, not *me* want coffee—*I* want coffee. Yes, I want coffee," as you pour yourself a cup. Don't correct his grammar. Simply rephrase what he has said. For example, if he said "Me want milk," hand him the milk as you rephrase the sentence to "I want more milk." This shows him you understand what he wants, and it gives him the correct grammar model without making demands on him.

Don't expect a child of this age to understand rules of grammar or to use words the way we adults do. The way he combines words will make sense to him, but will not be logical to us. When he says "No bed, Mom, no bed go," it makes sense to him. He has not yet learned our complicated rules for putting words together in the right order. (Some of us have trouble with these rules all our lives.) He may also say "mouses" instead of "mice," "goed" instead of "went," or "me" when he means "I." Saying such things is typical for children of this age, and these should not be considered errors. By three years, your child should have learned that:

1. People talk because they want other people to know what they are thinking and feeling.
2. Words are made up of individual sounds.
3. Sentences are made up of different words.
4. Talking is made up of words said in a standard order. (It is not "ride for a go," but "go for a ride.")

Voice Problems. A child is apt to imitate the voice he hears most, which is usually his mother's. If her voice is pleasant, clear, and expressive, then he will probably develop a similar voice. If she constantly nags or screams in a rough, harsh voice, then he may eventually develop a voice like that, too. Some preschool children strain their voices by trying to imitate a voice that is too high or too low for their age, or by screaming and yelling a lot. We all have a natural pitch level that we should use when talking. This is

based on the size of our vocal cords at a particular age. A voice problem can result if we use a voice that is much lower or higher than we should. This could happen to a little boy who tries to imitate a man's deep voice. Too much shouting can likewise be very harmful. Small boys and mothers are most often likely to do this. Constant yelling can irritate the vocal cords, producing growths on them similar to small warts or corns. Gradually these growths disappear if the person stops misusing his voice. Some growths, though, must be removed by surgery. Do you think your child's voice is extremely shrill, too soft, hoarse, or nasal (that is, it sounds as if it is coming through his nose)? If you do, then he should be seen by a medical doctor who specializes in ear, nose, and throat conditions (an otolaryngologist). If anyone—you or your child—has a voice change (like laryngitis) that lasts for two weeks or more, go immediately to an otolaryngologist. If the vocal cords continue to be misused, they may become permanently damaged.

Building Awareness. The directions that you give your child can now become more complicated. Ask him to do two or three things, one right after the other. You might say "Go out in the backyard by the doghouse, get your truck, and put it in the toy box." You can also talk about little details when you are looking at a picture or reading him a story. He may surprise you with the comparisons he makes. He is going to be using more words that have to do with feelings and ideas—like "nice," "fun," "happy." He should know his name and use the word "I" by the time he is three. He will keep touching things to find out what they are like, whether he is handling a new toy, the food he eats, or all the wonderful things to play with outdoors. He will be able to take things apart and put them together again. He may spend a half-hour or more at it.

Learning about the World. At about this age your child will be learning to get along with playmates. This means learning to share his toys and their toys. He will also be learning about safety limits. You must remind him of the rules about staying in the yard, not going into the street, and keeping away from animals or people he does not know. When he is between two and three, you should start to talk about his not going away with strangers. It isn't necessary to scare him. He will want to please you, but you must talk about it many times until you are sure he remembers.

Becoming a Person. It has been mentioned before how important it is for a child to develop good feelings about himself as a person. Developing these feel-

ings is related to developing a positive attitude toward one's sexual identity. Sexuality is the total expression of who you are as a male or a female. It is a process of becoming a man or a woman; it is not an act. It includes being self-confident, knowing who you are, and feeling okay about yourself.

How you feel and react when your child expresses interest and pleasure in his or her body will have a long-lasting effect on the development of his or her sexual identity. And so, when your children either ask you about their genitals or you want to tell them, give these parts their standard names. Since this is a time when your children are adding many new words to their vocabulary, why not start right from the beginning and teach words such as "penis" or "vagina," and sentences like "I have to urinate" or "I have to BM" ("bowel movement" will come later). When they use these words and sentences, all adults will be able to understand them. No one will have to figure out what "tee-tee," "poo-poo," or "doo-doo" is, or any other of the dozens of baby-talk words we use. Why we adults hesitate to give a two-year-old the standard words for these body parts or functions is something *we* should think about. Around this age, at one time or another, most children will be curious enough about themselves to ask what those body parts are—perhaps when taking a bath, using the toilet, or being dressed. When such a question is asked, why not answer it with the standard word? Remember, children at first have no words for *any* body parts or their uses. These are all learned. Since we do not give their noses, ears, and eyes special names, why do it for their genitals? If you calmly and easily give them the standard names and explain their uses when they ask, they will just as calmly and easily add them to their vocabulary and use them. This way, the body parts and functions will take on no special or upsetting meanings. This will help you both talk more directly and openly later.

A good self-image means not only that your child feels good about himself, it means he knows he is special. We know his feelings about himself begin to develop through the sounds of your voice and being touched. Your baby responds to you and your touching, stroking, and caressing from the moment he or she is born. It is most natural for children to respond to their own touch, to explore their own bodies—starting with their hands and fingers, then their toes, face, and genitals. For parents to know and accept this as something typical that most children do is an important step in the positive development of their children's sexuality. Allow this exploration as something that is natural and okay. Explain calmly when questions are asked. Do not scold or shame them when they explore their bodies, or the body of a little friend of the same or opposite sex. It is natural for them to be inquisitive about themselves and others, just as they are inquisitive about the rest of the world around them. This exploring and interest will not end with one explanation. Your child will be curious for a long time to come. Your understanding and acceptance when you find your child manipulating or fondling himself or herself is most important to his or her total development. Your attitudes and actions are most important in helping your child become a person who feels positive about himself and others.

QUESTIONS ON DEVELOPMENT

Answer the questions in this section. If you can answer "yes" to at least half of them, your child is probably developing typically. If you cannot, then answer the questions for the next youngest age group. Keep working back until you can answer "yes" to more than half the questions in a section. This will give you an *approximate* age level of development for your child.

TWO TO THREE YEARS: General

1. Does he use four words in an average sentence?
2. Is he beginning to understand number concepts like "one" and "many"? (For example, does he understand "Get me one block" or "Get me lots of blocks"?)
3. Does he listen to longer stories?
4. Can he identify seven pictures by hearing their names when you say "Find the _____"? (Fill in the blank with words like "dog," "cup," "shoe," "house," "flag," "clock," "star," "leaf," "basket," "book.")
5. Does he organize his thoughts and words to tell a story, share his ideas, or express his feelings?
6. Does he refer to himself by the word "I"?
7. Can people outside the family understand him, even though his speech isn't perfect?
8. Has his memory improved by now? (For exam-

ple, can he remember what happened yesterday, even though he may not completely understand words like "yesterday" and "tomorrow"?)

9. If you do ask him to bring you three of anything—books, toys, cookies—can he do it?

10. Does he learn from what he hears?

11. Can he tell you his first and last name?

JIMMY UH...
JIMMY SOMETHIN...,

12. Does he know how old he is and the name of the street where he lives?

13. Can he remember three directions at a time without your repeating them while he's doing them? (For example, "Shut the door, get your hat, and sit down" or "Pick up the chalk, draw a circle, and erase it" or "Pick up the books, give them to me, and sit down in your chair.")

14. Can he walk up steps without help?

15. Does he like to do things for himself?

16. Can he match some colors? (Show him something that is red, for instance, and ask him to find a color that is like it.)
17. Does he enjoy playing with other people?
18. Does he pay attention for at least seven minutes to any one activity, even though he may spend more time on activities he likes best?
19. Does he repeat two numbers after you've said them?
20. Does he share his feelings with you?
21. Does he talk to people he hasn't met before?
22. Is he toilet trained?

Physical Skills

1. Can he ride a tricycle using the pedals?
2. Can he put on his own shoes (except for tying them)?
3. Can he kick a ball?
4. Can he copy circles on paper?
5. Can he feed himself without too much spilling?

After answering these questions, you may feel anxious; a lot of parents do. Just remember that *these questions on development represent averages only. Each child is different, and there will be many variations within the limits of what is typical.*

If, according to the "Questions on Development," your child's development is a year or more behind his actual age, he may need some special attention. Talk to your pediatrician or a school psychologist if you have questions. You can also go to the well-baby clinic of a hospital or the local health department to get answers to your questions. You may also find help through United Way information services, a specialist in child development, or a good nursery or day-care center.

SUGGESTED ACTIVITIES

Self-Correction. (See Glossary) Self-correction is just what it says. You correct mistakes *you* make— not somebody else's. You can help your child learn to do his own correcting by occasionally making mistakes in your own speech and language, then casually correcting yourself. First be sure he is able to make the sound you are going to work on. (See the Sound Development Chart on page 219.) Use words with those sounds that are giving him particular trouble. For example, you might say ''Where is that 'poon'? No, not 'poon,' *'spoon.'* Where is that *spoon?''* Then go right on talking. This shows him that making a mistake isn't so bad, that everyone says words differently now and then. It also helps him hear the differences between sounds, and encourages him to try saying a word over that he may have said differently.

Following Directions. You can help your child listen to and follow directions by playing hiding games like ''I Spy'' or ''Hide the Thimble.'' Give him clues like ''You're close . . . you're going the wrong way . . . look up high. . . .'' He will be more successful if you begin by using large objects like a sofa pillow, book, or cigar box. Later, you can hide tiny things like candy, buttons, and little toys.

Most of us have a habit of talking too fast, at least some of the time. It helps your child hear the sounds that make up a word if you stretch them out like this:

"Show me your ssssock (sock)." "Show me your nozzzz (nose)." "Where is your carrrr (car)?" This will help him realize that words are made by putting sounds together in different ways, and will give him a chance to hear sounds he may not be using. A two-year-old is often fascinated by the way words sound alike, so join in when he's rhyming words together. If you hear him say something like "pay, day, may," add some more to his series, saying "way, say, hay." You may feel silly, but he will enjoy it.

Conversation. One of the most important ways you can help your child learn to talk is to talk *with* him—not *to* him. Spend some time just listening and talking with each other. Sometimes we forget that our children need to have listeners. Carry on a conversation with him in which you both have to listen a little and talk a little. Your example of taking turns will help him learn how useful talking is.

Extending Conversation. When you hear your child say "See car go," you may extend the conversation by saying "The car goes fast" or "See the car go fast." This will help him learn more words and use longer sentences.

Putting Words Together. Try these ideas to help your child learn how to put words together:

1. Remember that the word order he uses will be different from yours. If he says "Milk more, more me," simply say it over like this: "Billy wants more milk. Here's your milk." Let him hear the right word order, but don't make him repeat it. Just let him hear it the right way. In time, he will copy you.

2. When he uses a word in a very general way, you can then help him understand that he can use other words with more exact meanings. For instance, if he uses the word "drink" for all liquids, ask him "Do you want milk? or water? or juice?"

3. Use self-talk and parallel talk. As you give him a glass of milk, for instance, say "Billy wants to drink milk . . . Billy's drinking milk."

Looking. When you are out walking, it's a good time to look for flowers (and petals and stems); trees (and leaves, branches, roots, and bark); fences (and boards, nails, hooks, paint, and scratches); cracks in the sidewalk, and even tiny ants crawling there. Look for little things as well as big ones.

Listening. Have your child listen for hard-to-hear sounds around the house. Draw his attention to the sound of the refrigerator, keys and coins jingling in your pocket, the furnace, footsteps, or water dripping. Have him listen for hard-to-hear sounds outside. You might talk about the sound of a faraway airplane, the distant noises of cars or trucks passing on the road, leaves rustling, or the crack of branches. Make sure he knows what they are as you talk about them. You can help him learn to listen by talking about the different humming sounds the tires make or the high and low squeaks of branches rubbing together. It will help him understand the words and the meanings of "like" and "different."

Music. Most children of this age really like musical toys. If it's possible, let your youngster use a children's record player and a few inexpensive records. Try some march music and give him a wooden spoon, tin pan, and folded newspaper hat. Show him how to march and bang the pan. Then, join in once in a while and have a parade around the house.

Reading. Plan a regular time now each day for reading to your child. Use books that have a picture story that is interesting by itself without the printed story. Or choose a written story without any pictures that is exciting enough to hold his interest. If a book has both—good pictures and an interesting story— you can be sure it's a good one. A child likes to hear the same story again and again. This repetition will help him remember it. He will soon jump in and take part in telling the story himself. Playing children's records is another good way to have him hear stories. Remember, your library is probably a good place to get the right records for your child's age.

Pasting. Learning to paste may be messy, but it's fun. To make your own paste, take a handful of flour and add water—a little at a time—until the mixture is gooey. Then add a little salt. Be sure to make the paste thick enough so it won't run all over the paper. It won't be as sticky as commercial paste, but it will work. Help out, but let your child come up with some of his own ideas on what to paste together.

Painting. Give your two-year-old the opportunity to paint. Have him wear one of his father's old shirts or his mother's old blouses to cover his clothes. A one-inch paintbrush from the hardware store is much easier for him to handle than a small artist's brush. Lay paper flat on the floor or table and tape it down. Baby-food jars, muffin tins, or wide plastic bowls can be used to hold the paint. Thick, water-base paints are best. Because he may want to put just a bit of paint on each piece of paper, use cheap paper such as old newspapers or grocery bags. Start him out with

one color at a time. This lets him see just how each color looks. After he has painted this way for some time, let him start using two or three colors at the same time. When he's using more than one color, he may mix them together. You can show him how to wash out his brush between colors. He's likely to get a little messy and wet, but that's okay. He'll probably wind up with some interesting color designs.

Coloring. *"There is no "wrong way" to color a coloring book*. You just get better as time goes on. Coloring will help your child improve his hand-eye coordination. However he does it, it's okay. Don't pressure him to copy you or his older brothers and sisters. He will try to imitate you, so don't make it hard for him by being super-perfect when you color together. While coloring books are okay, plain paper is better because it lets his creativity blossom. He can draw and color whatever he wants. Plan on using both coloring books and plain paper, and when he is done, talk about his work. If you're not sure just what his creation is all about, ask him. You might insult him by talking about a cow that is really a picture of his mother or father! Be sure to use some parallel talk when he is coloring in a coloring book. Say something like "Billy's coloring the cow's horn. Now he's coloring an ear. Billy's making the tail blue." Keep building his self-confidence as he works.

Finger Painting. Two-to-three-year-olds usually like brush painting more than finger painting. However, some of them like having their hands in the paint and feeling it ooze through their fingers. Show your two- or three-year-old how to finger paint by spreading paint all over the paper and then making different designs with your fist, palm, or fingers. Almost any heavy paper with a smooth surface is good to use for finger painting. Shelf paper, a side from a

cardboard box, or paper plates are fine. You can mix your own paint. Here are a few ideas:

1. Add food coloring to liquid laundry starch. Mix to just the color you want.
2. Mix nonmentholated shaving cream with some powder paints or food coloring. The shaving cream will wipe off easily with a dry cloth or paper toweling, and is usually less messy than commercial or other homemade finger paints.
3. Try chocolate pudding. It feels so deliciously gooey—and you can eat it! Use it with wax paper on the kitchen table.

Don't forget to use some of your child's artwork to decorate the house. Generally, the kitchen is a good place to display it—especially the outside of the refrigerator. Everyone can see it there. Remember, it's important to let him know that you're proud of his work by hanging up his pictures and telling him you like them.

Scrapbooks. Keep making scrapbooks. (Review the material on page 95 on how to make scrapbooks.) Your child may now be able to help make his own by looking through old magazines to find pictures he likes. If possible, take photographs of him doing different things. Make up a series of pictures that tell a story about going to the store, the park, or a picnic. Then put these pictures in a scrapbook. This is another good way of developing his feelings about himself as a person. It also gives him a chance to talk to others when he shows them the scrapbook.

Flannel Board. A flannel board can add extra fun to telling stories. It also gives your child's imagination a chance to take over. You can buy a flannel board or make one yourself. Cover a piece of Masonite, fiberboard, or heavy cardboard with flannel. You can glue it on, or attach it with masking tape or cellophane tape that is sticky on both sides. Then cut different figures from colorful scraps of flannel. You can also attach little pieces of flannel to the backs of pictures. The bits of flannel or flannel-backed pictures will stick to the flannel board when you press them on. If you lay the flannel board flat, or place it at a slight angle, the pictures will stay where you put them.

Modeling Clay. Let your child play with clay or modeling dough. Playing with clay helps your child see things in three dimensions. Clay-modeling with your child will give you a chance to develop his sentence form and add more words to his vocabulary. You can also work on ideas such as "different," "alike," "top," "bottom."

Here are three different recipes:

1. 1 cup salt   2 tablespoons vegetable oil
   ½ cup water   A couple of drops of food coloring
   1½ cups flour

   Mix everything together.

   A small child can put this kind of clay in his mouth and it will not hurt him. Before he handles it, remember to dust his hands with flour so the dough won't be too sticky.

2. Pour soap flakes into a bowl. Stir in a tablespoon of water at a time until the soap is thick enough to model.

3. 1 part salt   1 part flour   ½ part water
   Mix everything together until soft and smooth. You can store the mixture in an airtight container in the refrigerator. Use it up within four days.

Mailbox. Children can put make-believe letters or picture cards in a toy mailbox and then deliver them to everyone in the family. You can make a mailbox out of a small cardboard box or grocery bag. Do a little decorating with red, white, and blue crayons. Then cut a slot in the side in which to put letters. Some toy mailboxes also have openings for different-shaped blocks that you put in the mailbox just as you would letters. Ideas such as "in," "out," "under," "round," and "square" can be taught by doing this with your child. If he "delivers" the "mail," it will give him a chance to talk to others and use more and longer sentences.

Lacing Shoe. Don't expect your child to learn to tie his shoes when he is two or three. But do give him one of his father's old shoes or a toy shoe to lace. Be sure the toe of the play shoe faces away from him so he learns to lace from the right direction. While he's

doing this, use such phrases as "lace the shoe," "in and out," and "up and over."

Sticker Books. These have press-out and stick-on parts with which your child can make or complete pictures. They may call for him to match up a pressed-out part with a figure outlined by a dotted line. Sticker books are fun, and a good way to develop a child's seeing skills. But don't expect your two- or three-year-old to use these books all by himself. He will need your help, with lots of parallel talk and self-talk to explain how to use them. Sticker books are a good "together" activity.

Large Toys. A wagon, tricycle, swing, or slide are large toys a two- to three-year-old child should have a chance to use. When a child plays with them, he is developing and improving the large muscle movements of his arms and legs.

Development and control of a child's large muscles and small muscles are happening at the same time. If you have tried the activities suggested so far, you are giving him a good balance of things to do for practice of both kinds. The muscles used for speech are fine muscles and take great control. After years of working with children and adults on communication problems, I am still amazed at the way speech and language processes develop. A typical child will go from the birth cry to words in a year, begin using sentences in two years, and by the age of five be able to talk his way out of more mud-puddle problems than you'd believe possible. This is truly amazing!

Child Management. Rewards are better than punishments for persuading your child to behave.

You have been using rewards all along, only we just didn't call them that. All those smiles, hugs, pats, cuddling, sitting close to you, and words of praise have been your child's rewards. When you deliberately don't give him those, because of something he did, he may think of that as punishment.

But sometimes holding back on rewards just isn't enough. If you feel you need something more to help manage your child, turn back to page 122 for some suggestions on what to do when he really acts up. (Believe me, there will be times when he will.) If you start now using severe punishment or spanking as your main method of making him do what you want, you will wind up losing some of his trust and confidence and making him feel bad about himself as a person. When he does get into mischief, try to figure out why. You will probably find a logical reason (logical for him, anyway). If you must spank, try not to lose control of your temper. Use only your hand.

Never hit him anywhere on or around the head. And one or two quick taps will be enough. Spanking should take place immediately after the act for which your child is being punished. It should never be done "when your father gets home" or "when your mother gets home." If you see something *about* to happen and you have already told him "no," a quick tap just ahead of what he was going to do will tell him that's a real "no-no."

Most preschoolers try very hard to please their parents, but some children have never been shown what *is* expected of them. They seem only to learn what they're *not* supposed to do. If you only notice your child when he's naughty, then he may act naughty to get your attention. To him, attention of this kind is better than no attention at all.

On the other hand, he can't have your attention whenever he wants it. You may sometimes have to tell him that you don't have time to spend with him. Say something like "Billy, I'm changing your sister's pants" or "I have to make supper." But please don't forget to return and answer his questions after you have finished changing those pants! And try not to make him wait *every* time he wants your attention.

Rewarding your child for talking will encourage him to talk more. Some rewards he will like and understand are:

1. Showing him that you understand what he says by smiling and nodding your head.
2. Getting him what he asks for (within reason).
3. Carrying on a conversation with him.
4. Sometimes giving him food treats, such as

raisins, peanuts, or an apple, when you two have had a good talk time.

Attention Span. Two-to-three-year-olds seem to be all "wiggle and go." That's fine. But it's also important to sit still long enough to hear a good story, or try a new puzzle, or explore an interesting toy (like a box that rattles and is hard to get open). Each of us comes equipped with different amounts of energy and inquisitiveness. If your little one is always on the go, and doesn't stay interested in one thing for a reasonably long period of time (say, twenty minutes or so) you may have to work at extending his attention span.

Watch your child at play, both in the house and out of doors, to find out what he takes a special interest in. It may be coloring, cutting, pasting, running, reading, climbing, digging, or making mud pies. Then join in and try to keep him interested for longer periods of time. This doesn't mean that you will sit with him for an hour or two at a time. His attention probably will not last that long. We are talking about taking ten minutes and making it fifteen, fifteen minutes and making it twenty. Bedtime is a good time to work on this. To help slow your child down, don't start roughhousing with each other just before bedtime. Instead, do things that will help quiet him down and get him ready for sleep. Try such things as working on a puzzle or reading a story. He may think he's putting one over on you because he's delaying his bedtime, but you're really accomplishing something useful. Just set a time that is long enough to extend his usual attention span. Then off to bed.

Three To Four Years

TYPICAL SPEECH AND
LANGUAGE DEVELOPMENT

When your child reaches this age, you may think he is talking *too* much! He not only talks a lot but he seems to be asking so many questions. A very typical three-and-a-half-year-old child may ask as many as 400 questions a day! He is trying out his talking skills and at the same time getting information. In addition, he knows this is a way to get your attention. The more his questions are ignored, however, the more questions he will ask. He is trying to get information when he asks questions, and you should answer him when this is the case. The problem is that children sometimes ask questions when they already know the answers. This is one way of starting and continuing a conversation with you.

You can usually reason with a three-year-old by talking to him. He should understand you better now, and you should have less trouble understanding him. His memory has probably improved. He should remember things that have happened in the recent past, though you can expect him to be confused by words

like "yesterday" and "tomorrow." Nevertheless, he is getting better at remembering and listening. This will make longer and more complicated stories more interesting to him.

He should begin to understand that words stand for feelings and ideas as well as things. Words like "good," "tired," or "cold" should have more meaning for him. He should be using more complex phrases like "under the bed," "in my dresser," "on top of the table," or "down in the basement." Words that sound alike will be less confusing for him, too. He should know the difference between the word telling what a bird does ("flies") and the "flies" buzzing around the garbage. He will use "I" at the beginning of a sentence rather than "me," and he may say "She took my car" instead of "Her gots my car." He will still make mistakes, like adding "ed" to all words telling about something that has already happened. He knows this useful rule, but may over-use it, saying "wented" for "went," "rided" for "rode," or "falled" for "fell." Children this age are also likely to be confused about what words to use to tell you about more than one of anything. They may say "foots" for "feet," or "mans" for "men." These confusions usually correct themselves if you continue to be a good model. Remember, *don't correct or criticize him*. Just repeat the words correctly and let it go at that.

Your child may be substituting sounds for the standard ones. For example, words like "very" and "bath" may be pronounced "berry" and "baf." The

sounds made by the letters "b" and "v," or by "th" and "f," are close enough for him to think they are the same. These are just differences in the sounds he uses, *not* mistakes or errors. Even with these differences, almost everyone should understand what he says by the time he is three years old. A three-year-old child who says "wabbit" for "rabbit" *does not* have a speech problem. On page 219 you will find a chart that tells you when you can expect your child to be able to use certain sounds. There are some things you just can't hurry. One of them is the fine muscle development that will let him say a difficult sound like "r," as well as many other sounds. Being able to coordinate his tongue, lips, teeth, jaw, and the roof of his mouth is very complicated. The way he hears things may also affect the way he says sounds. There are times you just have to wait for his body to grow and develop before he can do certain things, so have patience.

A three-year-old's talking vocabulary will average about 900 words, growing to 1,500 words by the time he is four. That's a lot of words. But don't expect your four-year-old child to talk like an adult. After all, the average adult uses between 12,000 and 13,000 words daily when he is talking, and a four-year-old just can't compete with that!

A child will discover that words are useful not only for getting information but also for controlling other people. He can say some words and people will do things. Making requests like "I want a cookie" or "I want to go too" seem to work. He might even give directions to himself or to his toys, then carry them out. He may also talk to imaginary playmates. These often appear in a child's life somewhere between two and four years of age, and usually disappear after five or six. If he doesn't have anyone to play with, or if he has an active imagination, he may "create" a friend. This is perfectly okay, and actually helps his language develop.

All the areas of development—seeing, hearing, touching, and feelings—are now more involved with one another and more closely related than before. His development of both large and small muscles is being coordinated with his thinking processes. He is learning how to cope with his world in many ways. Avoiding collisions on his tricycle, running round the backyard, and figuring out how to open the new lock on the yard gate (so he can get out and play where he knows he isn't supposed to) are all ways of doing this. He can handle longer sentences with three or four directions in them. He should also have a chance to play more difficult games that ask him to figure out whether things are alike or different. His seeing and touching skills should be built around games that ask him to look for fine details and really tiny differences. This will help him get ready for reading when he's asked to see differences in letters like "p," "d," and "b," or "m" and "w," or "n" and "u."

One more thing: Your child will be finding new friends to play with and learning from them. He is becoming more independent, and you may discover that he doesn't want to be held and cuddled as much because he is "growing up." This doesn't mean that all touching should stop. It just means he needs less of it because he feels secure and self-confident, and doesn't need close contact with you as constant reassurance. A smile or word of affection or praise can replace a hug or caress. Becoming independent is an important step in growing up. You can help him by *letting it happen*.

It is still necessary, however, to be consistent in setting limits. Your child will be learning many things from his playmates, and some of his actions and words may upset you. Remember, he is now able to reason more, so you can talk to him about such things as where he can and cannot play or using words that bother you. (He probably doesn't know their meanings.) Be sure he has a chance to use words that will let you and others know when he is happy, unhappy, annoyed, angry, or hurt. Being able to tell people that you are angry or unhappy is much better than hitting, biting, pushing, or kicking to let them know how you feel.

NORMAL NONFLUENCY

There is a time in your child's development when he will have what is called **normal nonfluency** (see Glossary). A three-year-old child will often repeat a sound like "s-s-s-s," or a "syl-syl-syllable" like that, or a word "like-like-like" this. Repeating, pauses, backing up, holding on to sounds, and general confusion of "thinking and talking" are very typical at this age. Children between three and four years of age have many experiences they want to talk about, but do not know how to put enough words together to express themselves smoothly. It is therefore easy to understand why their speech is like this during these years.

Too often, however, parents call this normal nonfluency **stuttering** (see Glossary). Stuttering *can* be a serious problem, but in my opinion it doesn't have to exist at all. The do's and don'ts that follow are the kinds of things that are very important in helping you avoid the problem of stuttering. As one who has seen so much unhappiness because of this problem, I can say that the proverb "An ounce of prevention is worth a pound of cure" fits perfectly.

There are definite ways for you to react to your child's nonfluency. These are the things that will reduce his chances of becoming a stutterer. They are all equally important.

1. Pay attention to your child when he talks to you. Let him know that you're listening. Give him your time and attention when he has something urgent to say. Remember that he wants to share his feelings, experiences, and ideas with you. Let him know that you are interested. Don't rush him.

HEY, MA LOOK!

2. If you are in the middle of a task, like doing the dishes, stop for a minute. Bend down so you and your child are on an eye-to-eye level, and listen. A little touch on the arm or scooping him close to you will let him know you are really listening. When a busy father comes home to sit down and read the paper or catch a few minutes of television, this may be the very moment your child takes to come running to tell you about his day. Put down the paper, turn away from the television, and pay attention to him. It won't take long. He'll be off and going soon, but the paper will stay right there and the news will be back on the television long after he has gone to bed.

3. Don't insist that he talk if he's crying, has hurt himself, or is obviously upset. These situations will almost always disrupt his fluency. Calm him down first. Comfort him and stop the heavy sobbing before you ask him what happened.

4. Don't put him on exhibition for relatives and friends by having him recite stories and little rhymes. Don't coax him to "say hello" or "tell the nice lady goodbye." When he feels like talking, he will. If you are concerned about his developing good manners, *just use them yourself!* Be his model and he will copy you.

5. Keep your own speech slow and easy to understand when you are talking to him. Let him hear talking that is easy for him to copy.

6. Don't interrupt him when he's talking, or complete his sentences out loud. He will not like your interruptions. All he wants is a good, attentive

listener. He shouldn't have to worry whether you'll let him finish.

7. Don't make suggestions to him about talking in a better way. *Never* make comments like "Slow down," "Think about what you are going to say," "Stop and take a deep breath," "Count to ten," or "Start over." This advice only gives a false idea that something is wrong with the way he talks. It makes him think that his speech is not good enough to please you. Comments like these won't help him stop his nonfluent speech. If anything, they will make him uncertain, upset, and more likely to develop into a stutterer.

8. None of us like to do things we feel we can't do well. Whenever possible, avoid situations where he will feel that he's failing. Encourage him to play games and to do things he does well. Don't make him compete with the kid next door. Don't tell him "Grow up," "Stop acting like a baby," or "You're the worst kid I've ever seen." The amount of nonfluency in his speech development will often depend on how he thinks about himself.

9. If he is frustrated and complains "I can't say that word" or "I can't talk right," then let him know, by explaining, that some words give you trouble too. Use an example of a word that's difficult for you to say—something like "linoleum," "chrysanthemum," or "aluminum." Sometimes use much easier words that he may have trouble with too. Convince him that you have trouble talking sometimes. (If you want to check this

out, have someone in the family count the number of times you say "ah" or "uh" when you are talking during mealtime.)

10. If he seems to become startled or upset by saying words nonfluently, you should calmly reuse the words in a natural and typical way. If he says "Billy broke my t-t-t-t-toy," you might say "Did he break your *toy?* Where is it? Let's go see if we can fix that old *toy*."

11. There will be days when things are going well and he is much more fluent. Take advantage of these times to let him talk. Suppose he comes in from playing, really wanting to talk and tell you what's been going on, and he starts out without any hesitations or repetitions. Join in by asking him to tell you all about it. Don't ask too many questions, though. Just let him go. Suppose however, he starts out with a lot of repetitions and hesitations. Then choose your questions carefully. Ask questions that take short answers. "Were you having fun?" (He can answer "Yes," "No," or "Uhuh.") "Who were you playing with, Billy or Mary?" In this instance, ask a question that will take a short, specific answer. Take the pressure off him so he won't have to struggle to tell you what's been going on.

12. Tell other people not to imitate or joke about his nonfluent speech. This includes his brothers, sisters, other relatives, friends, babysitters, and especially grandparents. Be very definite and outspoken about how you want others to talk to him when he is nonfluent.

13. *Never* discuss his nonfluency when he can overhear you. He should not be made to feel that the way he talks is special or wrong.

"SHE SURE HAS TROUBLE"

"SHE TALKED BETTER YESTERDAY."

"I DON'T KNOW WHAT'S THE MATTER WITH HER."

14. Changing a child from left-handed to right-handed does not cause stuttering. However, if you put pressure on him by insisting he try to make such a change, you may cause emotional problems. (See the section "Right-Handed or Left-Handed?" on page 103.) If you are still not sure whether he will be right-handed or left-handed, I suggest you ask a child psychologist or the psychologist at your local school to test him.

QUESTIONS ON DEVELOPMENT

Answer the questions in this section. If you can answer "yes" to at least half of them, your child is probably developing typically. If you cannot, then answer the questions for the next youngest age group. Keep working back until you can answer "yes" to more than half the questions in a section. This will give you an *approximate* age level of development for your child.

THREE TO FOUR YEARS: General

1. Do his sentences average four to five words?
2. Does he talk about things that haven't actually happened? (For example, does he say "Suppose that . . . ," or "I hope . . . "?)
3. Can he tell a story, even though he misuses some words and has some strange word combinations?
4. Does he ask a lot of questions, including questions to which he already knows the answers?
5. Can he repeat a sentence of eight or nine syllables? (Ask him to say "We are going to buy some candy.")
6. Can he name three colors?
7. Does he use plurals like "toys," "children," or "houses"?
8. Can he copy a square?
9. Can he repeat three to four numbers?
10. Can he button his coat (large buttons)?
11. Does he put on his shoes or boots with help?

Physical Skills

1. Can he cut with a pair of scissors?
2. Can he catch a ball?
3. Can he hop by himself, making three hops on either foot?
4. Can he skip by himself?

5. Can he walk on a balance board without help?

After answering these questions, you may feel anxious; a lot of parents do. Just remember that *these questions on development represent averages only. Each child is different, and there will be many variations within the limits of what is typical.*

If, according to the "Questions on Development," your child's development is a year or more behind his actual age, he may need some special attention. Talk to your pediatrician or a school psychologist if you have questions. You can also go to a local school, health department, or the outpatient clinic of a hospital to get answers to your questions. You may also find help through United Way information services, a specialist in child development, or a good nursery or day-care center.

SUGGESTED ACTIVITIES

For the child three to four years old, there are many things you can do during almost any activity or at any time of the day to help his speech and language develop.

1. Use self-talk and parallel talk. (See page 90 for description.)
2. Be a good speech and language model for your child to copy. (See page 89.)
3. Up to now, the game of imitation has played a big part of his "ways to learn." It is just as important to keep this going now as it has been during his earlier growth and development.
4. Continue to praise and reward his speech and language efforts.

5. Talk with him as much as possible, so he has a chance to practice and improve his talking skills.
6. Work on extending his conversation. (See page 140.)

Word Order. Help your youngster learn to put words in the right order by using those words that give him trouble. Teach a better word order by your example. He may say "Me no go" or "I not go." This is quite typical for a three-year-old child. Help him learn a more acceptable order by saying to him "I don't want to go either." *Remember not to correct or criticize him.* Just repeat whatever he says in a different way. You are his model and if you keep repeating it your way, as well as using self-correction, he will begin to imitate you, saying the words and sentences the way you want him to.

Learning to use "I" instead of "me" sometimes takes quite a while. Try self-correction when he is with you. Talk loud enough for him to hear you. If he is watching too, that's best. Say something like "Me have to cook dinner now. No, not *me* have to cook dinner, *I* have to cook dinner. Yes, *I* have to cook dinner now." Stretch out the word "I," and say the whole sentence at least twice.

Word Associations. Continue to teach your child the relationship of words, objects, and ideas by talking about the ways they are alike and the ways they are different. Say "Here are two dogs. This one is white and this one is black." Or say "Look at the tables. There is a little table and here is a big table." Cut out pictures on one subject (like houses) and paste them in a scrapbook. Talk about how people live in different houses—big houses, small houses, wooden houses, brick houses, apartment houses. Mention how the houses are alike and how they are different. Do the same kind of thing with cars, airplanes, people, animals, trees, flowers, clothes, or anything else that is interesting to you or especially interesting to him.

Remember that if you do things that are interesting to *him*, you will be better able to extend his attention span. This will be especially helpful when he starts school, not long from now. (He may already be going to nursery school.) He will need that longer attention span when he is expected to sit still and listen, or even to lie still and relax at rest time.

Telling Stories. Tell stories together. Begin a story, then let your child take over after a short time. When he runs out of ideas, you take over and keep it going. (If one of you is apt to go on too long, set a time limit.) Here are some variations of this idea:

1. Make up stories about magazine pictures.
2. Make up a sentence about each picture.
3. Use a flannel board to tell a story.
4. Cut out a series of three or four pictures that make up a story. (Try the comic section of a newspaper.) Paste them on separate pieces of cardboard. Next, you make up a story about what's happening. Then let him try. First let him tell the story you have told. Later, let him tell his own story. Mix up the pictures sometimes to see if he can arrange them in the right order before he tells the story.

Asking Questions. There may be times when your

child really pesters you with questions and you would like to say "Stop bothering me" or "I'm too busy." If this happens a great deal, perhaps you should ask yourself why. Have you gotten so busy that you don't have time for him? If you are really that busy, can you shift things around so that his father (or mother) can take over and spend a little more time with him? The *amount* of time you spend with him is not as important as *how* you spend your time with him. If you take out just a few minutes at a time throughout the day, you can keep him from feeling left out or unimportant. His self-confidence and feelings about himself are still tender and fragile. He needs your support and reassurance. Make sure that these moments together are really *together,* without a lot of interruptions.

If your child asks question after question and you need some time off, the following suggestions might help:

1. Answer his questions with a question. If he says "What's this thing?" ask him "Is it big?" or "Is it little?" or "Is it a cup?" or "Is it a doll?" Make sure you suggest something quite different from what it is. You have simply asked him to answer his own question. Suppose he asks "Where are my shoes?" You might answer "Would they be in the oven?" This is good for a laugh, and it forces him to try to give a more logical answer. This silly but useful sort of game is something *you* should start every now and then. Ask questions like "Do airplanes eat ice cream?" (If they don't, who does eat ice cream?)

"Do you put your shoes on your ears?" (If you don't wear shoes on your ears, why not?) He may ask a question like "Why don't trees grow in the house?" This is your cue to ask questions that will make him figure out why they don't. You might say "Let's see, what do trees grow in? Is there any of that in the house? How big do trees get? How big is a house?"

2. Send him away to find the answer to his question. Suppose he has asked if it is going to rain. Then you can say "If there are clouds in the sky—big, dark clouds—it might rain. Go and look out the window and see if there are any big, dark clouds. Look all over the sky." Be sure you ask questions or make suggestions in all seriousness. Don't sound sarcastic or mad. And be reasonably sure he can come up with the answer.

Playing with Other Children. Children need to play with each other. They learn much about speech, lan-

guage, and just getting along by being with each other. If there are no other children nearby, think about sending your child to a preschool program such as a day-care nursery or a co-op nursery school. Early play with small groups of children, either family members or neighborhood children, is important. Whether he goes into a preschool setting or kindergarten, he will suddenly find that he has to share and get along with as many as 20, 30, or more children of his age. This is a big adjustment for many children. For some, it's very difficult. Letting your child learn to share, to give and take, to get along, is much easier if you begin with small groups and work up to the larger ones.

Reading. The stories you read to your child can now be a little longer and more complicated. Your public library is the best source of books for children. You can provide children with a whole new world of experience just by taking the time to visit and borrow books from the library. There's no expense involved. The public library offers its books and services free of charge. (For planning your child's first library visit, see page 232.)

When you go to the library, let him help pick out his books. If there's a children's librarian there, ask her to help you. His first visit will be an exciting, new experience for him. He is going to meet other people who are interested in him and he will see other children doing the same thing he is doing. He will also have the thrill of exploring a place that's very different from his home. There will be a lot to discuss, so talk about it before, during, and after his visit.

Drawing and Tracing. Have your child trace around simple shapes like blocks, cups, cookie cutters, or his hand. Tracing a picture through very thin paper is another drawing activity he can try. Drawing, coloring, and cutting out these shapes will help him see differences in colors, shapes, and sizes. It will give him practice in hand-eye coordination as well. A chalkboard is a good place for both of you to play dot-to-dot games. Draw two dots on the chalkboard and ask him to connect them. Then add another dot, and have him draw a chalk line to that point. Keep just one dot ahead of him. After he learns to draw short lines, put the dots farther apart and make the designs more complicated.

Painting. Let your child use small watercolor paint brushes. He can easily handle several colors at one time. You can buy some watercolor paints in spillproof jars. (This is not only easier on your floor but on your temper as well.) Save all your paper bags and wrappings to keep him supplied. Don't forget to put up some of those pictures when they are done. Help him print his name somewhere on the front where it can be seen.

Pasting. Have your youngster make designs by pasting ripped or cut paper, dry cereals, macaroni, wood chips, cloth, rice, seeds, or old buttons onto a large sheet of paper. This is a good rainy-day activity, and it's great for letting his imagination take over.

Macaroni. Paint the short, round kind of macaroni with holes that go all the way through. Let it dry. Then have your child string an old shoelace or piece of yarn through the macaroni to make a necklace, belt, or bracelet. You can work on groups or units. Put all the blues together, or all the reds together, or all the greens together. Or you can group three blues, four reds, five greens, and so on.

Paper Chains. You can buy craft sets for making paper chains. Better yet, you can make your own by cutting colored construction paper in strips six inches long and about one-half inch wide. Or cut similar strips from colored pictures in a magazine. Show your child how to form the first link by pasting the ends of a strip together. Then have him put the next strip through it and paste that one together, and so on for as many links as he needs. You can "design" the chain you are making by putting the strips in color combinations like six greens, three reds, and four blues, then repeating the pattern. A small picture can be pasted on each strip first. When the chain is finished, he can name the picture on each link. He can use the finished chain to decorate his room.

Sewing Cards. Sewing cards are made of sturdy cardboard with holes punched along the outline of a picture. Yarn is then pulled in and out through the holes. You can make your own sewing cards. Cut a simple, colorful picture from a magazine or catalog. Paste it on a piece of cardboard. Use a paper punch or a large nail to outline the picture with holes. Wrap cellophane tape or masking tape on the end of a piece of yarn, as on the tip of a shoelace. This makes the yarn easier to pull through the holes. Dipping the yarn ends in fingernail polish will also work.

Helping. Helping with little jobs around the house can be exciting to a three- or four-year-old. Ask yours to try washing a window, dusting, sweeping, wiping dishes, or setting the table. Don't expect him to do things perfectly. Plan on redoing them later

(when he's not around) if his work isn't up to your standards. The important thing is to make your child feel he has helped. He did the job the best he knew how. Don't be critical. A little praise for his good work will go a long way and he will want to "help" again. If you criticize him for the mess he makes, he will lose interest in helping at all.

Sorting. Children of this age often like to sort things. If you have old buttons, let your youngster sort them by size or color. Mix up two types of beans (or corn kernels and sunflower seeds) and let him sort them out. Let him sort his socks from his father's

bigger socks. Cut out some paper shapes for him to sort. If you cut them from different colors, he can sort them by color at first and later by shape. Try to keep the sorting jobs simple.

Shadow Pictures. Three-year-olds enjoy seeing their own shadows and the shadows their toys make. To make a good shadow picture, turn off the overhead lights. Leave on only one bright light. Stand your child between the light and a plain, light-colored wall where he can see the shadow pictures.

Mirror Image. I hope you have a mirror in your house that is large enough to let you and your child stand in front of it. When you do, just touching his shoulder and talking about how big he is getting to be will do much for his self-confidence and self-image. It will also let him see himself as others see him. If you have a dresser mirror, stand him on a chair or hold him up to it.

Puzzles. Your child may now enjoy making some of his own puzzles. Have him paste a picture on heavy cardboard. Cut the picture into pieces after the paste dries. Don't cut the pieces too small at first. The puzzle can always be cut into more pieces if it turns out to be too simple. It doesn't have to be cut in a complicated way like a jigsaw puzzle. Four to six simple pieces are plenty to start with. You can use plain construction paper and cut oblongs, squares, and triangles (but not all of them in one puzzle). Remember, puzzles are more fun when shared.

Fishing Games. Many toy companies make fishing games. You can also easily make your own set by cutting fish out of heavy paper or cardboard. Paste a picture on each fish and attach a paper clip or staple to its nose. Use a shallow box for a fish pond. Tie a heavy string on a stick and tie a magnet to the end of the string. The metal paper clip or staple on the fish will be attracted by the magnet and stick to it. As your child pulls in the fish, he can name each picture, listen as you name it, count his fish, talk about the pictures, or just have the fun of pretending to catch a fish.

Objects for Crawling and Climbing. Do you remember when you were little how much fun it was to make a house or hiding place by throwing a sheet or lightweight blanket over a card table or a couple of kitchen chairs? Try it. Your child will like it too!

Things to Use in Building. A favorite way to play at this age is to build things out of blocks, shoe boxes, milk cartons, cigar boxes, spring-type clothespins, Tinker Toys, large appliance boxes, or clean cans (with labels removed and one or both ends neatly and smoothly cut off). All of these activities call for imagination.

Coordination Games. Here are some games that take a certain amount of physical coordination:

1. *Ring-toss game*. Throwing large rings over a peg. This is not as easy as it looks.
2. *Beanbag game*. Throwing a small beanbag at a hole in a target or into a bushel basket.

3. Dropping clothespins into an open milk carton.

Be sure to start out at an easy level. If your child has trouble, have him stand closer to the target or make the opening larger. Help him be successful in these games. You can make the game harder as he improves. For more information on coordination games, see the book *Success Through Play* by Radler and Kephart (mentioned in the list of "Books for Parents" on page 240).

Dressing Up. Three- to five-year-olds find dress-up clothes are fun to wear. Old hats, shirts, dresses, shoes, suits, and pants are useful in helping your child play creatively. He can play "grown-up." (You may even see yourself in the way he acts during these masquerades.) It will give him a chance to try talking more like an adult.

This is an age when little boys will want to play with dolls and other toys that used to be considered girls' toys, and little girls will want to play with trucks, bats, balls, and other toys that at one time were considered little boys' toys. It is good if they each have a chance to play with any and all toys and games that were at one time considered suitable only for one or the other. This helps in the development of the child's sexual identity, his total self. It's very important to become aware of differences and to know that being different is okay. No child should ever get to feel that being different has anything to do with being better or worse, or right or wrong.

We have often talked about teaching children to know when things are alike and when things are different. We have done this by talking about things. Now we must do the same thing about *people*. This may be the hardest puzzle a child has yet to figure out—how in many ways people are alike, and in other ways different. Some people are girls; some people are boys. Some are men; some are women. Some are tall; some are short. Some always seem angry; some always seem happy. One great thing little children have in common: they accept all people, regardless of differences.

Child Management. Imitation and following a model are important parts of your child's learning. He imitates you. You are the model. If his parents or his brothers and sisters shout a lot or hit one another, he may do this also. If people hit him or yell at him a lot, this may be the way he will act with his playmates. If he has a friend who hits, pushes, or bites to get what he wants, you will have a teaching job to do with both of them when they're on your home ground. Remember, you can establish rules of play because it is your backyard or front porch or home, and *your child.* If a visiting child hurts your child by biting, hitting, or pushing him, or in any other way, send the other child home immediately. Let him know he cannot play with your youngster or any of his toys if he acts that way. Don't talk about his being a good boy. Just send him home or away immediately. If your child has done the biting, hitting, or pushing, treat him in the same way, just as quickly. Remove him from the play area and the group he's playing with. When he discovers that his friends continue to have a good time without him, he will learn that these are not effective ways to get what he wants or to have fun.

If the hitting, biting, and kicking take place between brothers and sisters, the same rules apply.

Stop the action. Find out what happened. Use the same methods of child management you have been using up to now (see page 148). Above all, *be consistent*. Being consistent means you treat each child equally when listening to an argument and settling fights. It also means you match your handling of the matter to the problem. If it is a minor problem, like who gets the biggest piece of cake, you make sure everyone gets a chance at being first to choose. If someone has been hurt, that is more serious. Whatever is decided, it should be discussed between parent and child before action is taken.

For a further discussion of child management and discipline, see the chapter "One More Time," beginning on page 205.

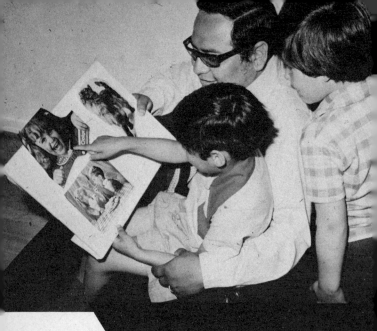

Four To Five Years

TYPICAL SPEECH AND LANGUAGE DEVELOPMENT

Your child should have completed about ninety percent of the job of learning how to talk somewhere between his fourth and fifth birthdays. He should have mastered the basic skills necessary to communicate, although it will take time for him to achieve the last ten percent of our adult speech and language skills. For help in understanding this, look at the section that describes the developmental levels of speech sounds on page 217.

Your child may not be saying all his sounds the way we adults say them. That's okay. There are many reasons for this, so don't become upset if he isn't talking just like you. If you have any questions, contact someone at your local school and ask for help. Since your child will start school soon, the school may plan a preschool screening program that will help answer your questions. If there is no preschool screening program in your area, contact the school anyway and ask to see a specialist in speech therapy or the school psychologist. Other sources of help are well-baby clinics at hospitals and your local health department. You may also find answers through United Way information services, a specialist in child development, or a good nursery or day-care center.

A four-year-old should be able to understand most of what you say when you speak in a typically adult manner. This does not mean that you can start reading Shakespeare or the encyclopedia to him! It does mean, however, that he will understand you now if you talk to him in almost the same way you would talk to an adult. At this age he needs to learn from a more complicated model, just as he needed a simpler model when he was much younger.

Talking experiences such as using the telephone, describing objects, and telling stories will give him the chance to learn new words and to combine them in a usable way. His talking vocabulary will have increased to about 1,900 words by the age of four and a half, and to 2,200 words by the time he is five. A typical adult with a high school education has more than 10,000 words in his speaking vocabulary. That's much more than the 2,200-word vocabulary of a five-year-old. However, the typical five-year-old will make good use of these words. But he needs to learn more words and their meanings, and he needs your help.

By the way, there probably will be a few words in his vocabulary that you may wish were not there. Children of this age will say things like "dirty pee-pee" and "poopie pants," and will often use "four-letter words" that most people disapprove of. Many of these will be expressions he has learned from other children, but you may hear a few words that sound familiar because you have used them yourself!

Even though a four- to five-year-old does a fairly good job of talking, he still has limited speech and language abilities. When we compare a four-year-old's conversation with that of an adult, we notice that his sentences are shorter and there is a more limited exchange of ideas. He may still be confused about how some words are used. For example, he may say "I don't want none" instead of "I don't want any." He may also have trouble adding the correct endings to words and making some of the more difficult sounds. All this is typical for his age, so be prepared for it.

Remember that your child will understand a great deal more than he is able to say. Remember, also, that you have spent a great deal of time and effort developing his imitation skills. You have worked hard at being his model, and now is no time to stop and rest. He needs more difficult questions and challenges. In turn, he will ask you more difficult questions and present you with greater challenges. Learning by seeing, hearing, and touching will go on for the rest of his life. Development of his muscle coordination will continue for many years, too.

Soon your child will be ready for a new skill. He will learn how to read. To do this, he must learn to recognize those many different written and printed shapes called letters. He must understand that letters stand for different sounds, and that they can be put together to form words. Words are put together to form sentences. When we say sentences out loud, we

call this talking. When we can figure out what written
and printed words and sentences mean, we call this
reading. Reading can and should be a fun thing to do.
If your child has had fun hearing you read to him or
looking at books during his earlier years, this will
help him discover the fun of reading.

Your child's self-image and self-confidence should
be well developed now. He's just about ready to
tackle the world. This means that he will think of

more things to get into than a barrel of monkeys. It
also means that there is no one else exactly like him
anywhere in the world. This is true even if he is a
twin or triplet. Remember that boys and girls come in
every shape, size, and kind imaginable. Whether you
have a boy or a girl, I hope you will encourage your
youngster to be himself or herself.

By now, your child-management methods should
be pretty well established. They began with your re-

sponse to your child's birth cry. In the years ahead, they will depend even more on his ability to communicate. His ability to communicate has become more than combining sounds and saying words. He can now express ideas. How he does this depends on his self-confidence, self-image, and understanding of himself. It further depends on how he feels about you, and whether he has learned to trust you and others.

All these things are very important in helping your child learn to get along with people. Learning to get along, or learning to live together, or learning to cope—call it what you want. It depends on his ability to communicate. Child management is now giving way to adult management. Learning how to get along, or how to cope—all his "how-to" learning— will be easier if his communication skills are well established and his feelings about himself are good and positive.

QUESTIONS ON DEVELOPMENT

Answer the questions in this section. If you can answer "yes" to at least half of them, your child is probably developing typically. If you cannot, then answer the questions for the next youngest age group. Keep working back until you can answer "yes" to more than half the questions in a section. This will give you an *approximate* age level of development for your child.

FOUR TO FIVE YEARS: General

1. Can he define four or more common words and tell something about how they are used? (Examples: hat, shoe, book, stove, dish, table, and house.)
2. Does he help with simple household tasks? For example, does he set the table?
3. Can he count to ten out loud?
4. Does he talk with very few sound errors? (See the section "Speech Sounds" on page 217.)
5. Does he ask questions to get information or explanations of word meaning, rather than just for something to do?
6. Does he spend time looking at books and enjoy having somebody read to him?
7. Can he name a penny, a nickel, and a dime as he points to them?
8. Does he say things like "Hello," "Hi," "Thank you," and "Please"? Does he make requests of others by saying "Do this" or "Get that"?
9. Does he sing simple songs?
10. Does he know the difference between boys and girls?

11. Does he take turns during group play?
12. Does he share his toys?
13. Can he move around his neighborhood alone?
14. Does he understand how far from home you allow him to go?

Physical Skills

1. Can he jump rope with others?
2. Can he dress and undress with little help (except to tie his shoes)?

3. Does his drawing of a wagon or a triangle resemble yours?
4. Does he stay mostly within the lines when coloring simple pictures?

If you can't answer "yes" to all these questions, you may feel anxious; a lot of parents do. Just remember that *these questions on development represent averages only. Each child is different, and there will be many variations within the limits of what is typical.*

If, according to the "Questions on Development," your child's development is a year or more behind his actual age, he may need some special attention. Talk to a school psychologist or perhaps your pediatrician if you have questions. Your local health department or the outpatient clinic of a hospital can often help you. Remember again, you may also get help through United Way information services, a specialist in child development, or a good nursery or day-care center.

SUGGESTED ACTIVITIES

A four-year-old should know how to make most speech sounds, how to put them together to make words, and how to put words together to make phrases or sentences. I hope that you will talk to your child whenever possible. That may sound simple, but few of us really do it. Say more than just "Uh-huh," "I see," and "Oh, yes." Really *listen* to what he says. Then answer with something more meaningful than those absent-minded responses we all tend to use with our children. It doesn't matter to him that you have to leave right away, or that the car needs new tires, or that you don't know what in the world to have for dinner. He is interested in telling you that Sally cut her knee. You might show your interest by saying "That's too bad. How did it happen?" Or, if he is telling you about the afternoon he spent playing with his friends, you might say "I'll bet that was fun. Did you have a good time?" Be interested in *whatever* your child says. Try to respond with comments that show you are listening and you care. Try to extend his conversation whenever possible.

Television. I hope you decide which programs your child will watch. Plan another activity when you don't want him to watch TV. Don't be afraid to turn the set off. When you can, make the choice as painless as possible, but if it comes down to a crunch decision, then stick to that decision. Avoid television programs that show violence. Set time limits. Remember that when your child watches television he is isolated and passive, not really involved with other people and activities. Don't put a television set in his bedroom. Encourage outdoor play with others. And keep playing that old-fashioned game of talking with each other!

Reading. Keep on reading to your child! Fairy tales and classic children's stories offer different and new worlds of adventure. Help him learn about them. By now he should know that books are interesting. If you have helped him learn that reading is fun, he will be more eager to learn to read than a child who has not shared books as he has.

Children's Magazines. If your child likes books and magazines, then try to get him his own. There are several magazines just for children. Some of them are:

Humpty Dumpty's Magazine
Parent's Magazine Press
80 Newbridge Road
Bergenfield, N.J. 07621
$6.95 per year (10 issues).
Digest size.
Things to do, stories to read to children, puzzles, games.
For ages 3-7.

Ebony, Jr.
Johnson Publishing Company
820 South Michigan Avenue
Chicago, Ill. 60605

$7.00 per year (10 issues).
Things to do, puzzles, stories, feature articles,
sights and sounds of the black community, calendar
of important dates.
For ages 5-12.

Young World (formerly *Golden Magazine*)
% *The Saturday Evening Post*
P.O. Box 6567B
Indianapolis, Ind. 46206

$6.95 per year (10 issues).
Stories, poems, things to do, puzzles.
For ages 4-10.

Jack and Jill
% *The Saturday Evening Post*
P.O. Box 6567B
Indianapolis, Ind. 46206

$6.95 per year (10 issues).
Stories, poems, simple science and nature articles,
puzzles, things to make.
For ages 4-10.

For more information on children's magazines,
look at *A Parent's Guide to Children's Reading* by
Nancy Larrick (see "Books for Children," page
233). And, above all, don't forget your public library.

Pasting. Your four-year-old should continue pasting. He can add leaves, dried flowers or weeds, dried
beans, rice, buttons, and small shells to his designs.
At this age, he is less likely to put things in his mouth,
and these things give him a chance to be more imagi-
native.

Cutting with Scissors. Your four-year-old can learn to handle scissors. Give him the blunt kind at first. Let him cut up old newspapers just for fun. He can cut outlines of simple shapes later on. Buy left-handed scissors if he is left-handed.

Clay Modeling. Your child will be able to make more things out of clay. Show him how to lengthen a piece into an oblong shape and how to attach lumps of clay together to make human or animal figures. Then give him pipe cleaners to insert for arms or legs. These can be cut into different lengths with large scissors or wire cutters.

Try making letters out of clay. Work especially on those that may cause trouble in reading: "b," "d," and "p"; "n" and "u"; "m" and "w." Seeing these shapes in three dimensions can help him learn to recognize them. Pipe cleaners can be used for making letters also.

For a dollar you can buy enough pottery clay from an art-supply store to get you started. This clay can be used for a long time if you store it in a plastic bag. Just sprinkle water in the bag now and then to keep it moist. You can also use this recipe for homemade clay and save the cost of buying it:

One cup of flour
One cup of salt
Mix with enough water to make a stiff dough.

This clay can be baked and then painted. It must be handled carefully because it breaks easily.

Water Play. Playing with water is still fun at this age, and it can also be instructive. Use a little food coloring and clear plastic containers of different sizes and shapes, and let your child discover how the same amount of water looks when it is poured from one container to another.

Coloring and Drawing. A four-year-old child should have a good idea of what he wants to draw. The shapes and colors may still be strange, but don't criticize. Say something like ''I like the way you gave that cat one red ear and one purple ear.'' This will increase his confidence, even if you wonder about some of his color choices. Hang up his pictures, and be sure that both his parents look at them and comment approvingly.

Give him paper plates, laundry shirt cardboards, newspapers, or plain paper for drawing and coloring. Show him how to place wax paper over the comics in the newspapers and rub the wax paper with a spoon. The picture will come off on the wax paper.

Draw an outline of your child as he lies on a large

sheet of wrapping paper. Let him paint or color the figure you have made. Then cut it out and hang it on the wall where the whole world can see it. Put up photographs of him and other members of the family also.

Puppets. Homemade or commercially made puppets can give your child a chance to be creative. They will help him let his emotions come to the surface more freely. With puppets, children can talk in new and different ways and can pretend to be someone other than themselves. Listen carefully. You may hear yourself!

You can buy many kinds of puppets. Puppets just as good, however, can be made at home. Here are some examples of the kinds of homemade puppets that your youngster can enjoy:

Paper Bag Puppets. Help him draw a face on a small paper bag. Cut the mouth out so that he can put his finger through the hole to look like a tongue.

Clothespin Puppets. Paste pictures of animals or people on a clothespin. Hang a sheet over a clothesline and clip the clothespin puppets to the line.

Pencil and Spool Puppets. Cut out pictures of people or animals from magazines or books. Paste them on empty thread spools. Make hair or beards out of yarn pieces or cotton. Add your own ideas too. Slip the spool over a pencil.

Old Sock and Mitten Puppets. You can make puppets of old socks and mittens. Draw a face on the sock or mitten with a crayon, sew on buttons for eyes, and use yarn for hair. Put your hand into the mitten or the toe of the sock. Make the puppet talk by moving your thumb up and down against the other fingers. The mouth looks as if it's opening and closing.

You can take the stuffing out of worn-out soft toys and use these as hand puppets too.

Sewing. Some four- to five-year-old children like to sew. If yours has learned to lace in and out of the holes on a sewing card, he can now begin to sew with a large needle on scraps of material. Help him learn to thread a needle and teach him how to stitch. At first children want to sew just for the pleasure of knowing how, so don't ask him to make anything in particular. By the time they are five, many children want to make things like pot holders, purses, and doll clothes. Boys of this age enjoy sewing too. Your boy won't be a sissy if he does. Some day he will appreciate knowing how to sew on a button!

Concentration. There are many ways you can play this game. Begin simply. Put three little toys (a car, a truck, and a ball, for example) on the table. Let your child look at them for a few seconds and then have him close his eyes while you take one object away. Then have him open his eyes and see if he can tell you which one you took away. As he gets better at this, you can add to the number of things on the table. You can also change the game around. Start with two or three toys, and *add* one instead of taking one away when he closes his eyes. Then when he opens them, he has to pick out the item you added.

You can use many things besides toys for this game. Try these: articles of clothing or food; household objects; coins; squares, circles, and triangles cut from construction paper or made from clay. Just about anything will work.

As your child gets better at the game, you can lay out five or six picture cards for him to name. Ask him to close his eyes while you take one away and hide it. He must then open his eyes and tell you what picture is missing. If he guesses right, then he gets to take an object or picture off the table while you close your eyes. A variation of this game is to cut off some part of a picture (a leg, wheel, or ear, for instance) and have him guess what part is missing.

For another variation, make or find pairs of matching pictures. Start with three sets (six pictures in all). Spread them out on the table and let your child look at them face up. Then turn the pictures upside down and mix them up. The object of the game is for each player to turn over a matching pair of pictures. Let your child turn over the first two pictures. If they are a matched pair, he can take them off the table and continue by turning over another two pictures. If the first turn does not produce a matched pair, the pictures are turned face down in their original places, and it is your turn to try for a matched pair. The idea is to help your child remember which are the matching pictures, so don't end up capturing all the cards yourself!

The game of concentration, with all its variations, can be fun for the whole family. If you are in doubt, always start with fewer items. You can make the game harder as your child gets better at it.

Talk Box. Collect small objects like those from gum-ball machines or Cracker Jack boxes and keep them in a special box called a "talk box." Hold the box up high and have your child reach in and take out an object. Then have him name it. When he gets to know what's in the box, have him close his eyes when he takes out an object, and let him guess what it is by handling it without seeing it. After a while, you

can add new things to the box without letting him know what they are. Take turns. Let your child be in charge while you do the picking and guessing. This game will help develop skill in recognizing shapes and sizes.

Word Games. There are many picture-word games played much like bingo. The ones listed here can be found in most dime stores or toy departments: "Simple Object Bingo" by Whitman; "Go Together Lotto Games" by Ed-U-Cards; "Slate Bingo" by Winthrop-Atkins Company, Inc.; "A to Z Lotto" by Standard Toykraft.

Categories. Play word games that help your child learn categories. An example: "What kinds of animals live on a farm? . . . in a jungle? How many different kinds of fish can we think of? . . . pieces of furniture?" Help him by naming some yourself.

Scrapbook. Here is something new to add to your scrapbook. If your child seems to have trouble saying some sounds, set aside three or four scrapbook pages. On the first of these, paste pictures that start with the sound you wish to work on. On the next page or two, add pictures that end with the sound. On the last page, put pictures that have the sound in the middle. Use this order with most sounds. It is usually difficult for a child to hear the sounds in the middle of a word. Start with pictures for words that are one syllable long. If you are working on the "sh" sound, choose words like "shoe" and "fish." These words show you the sounds he will be working on at the beginning and at the end. This will make it easier for him to hear the sound. Gradually you can add more difficult words of several syllables, such as "flash-light" or "undershirt."

Using the Telephone. A child of four or five should be able to use the telephone if necessary. Teach your youngster how to answer the phone and to find out who is calling. Teach him also how to call the local operator or emergency number. You may have occasion to be glad you did! Exlain to him that the telephone is not a plaything, and must be used only in a real emergency. Have make-believe telephone conversations with him to help him learn exactly what you want him to do.

Learning to Listen. I have often used a simple three-step way of helping a child learn to listen. It goes like this:

1. Talk about a sound you want to help your child hear; let's say it is "r." Make the "r" sound by stretching it out ("errrr"). Then hold up a picture, of a jar, perhaps, and say "jarrrrr," holding on to the "errrrr" sound. Ask him if the "r" in that word sounded like the "r" sound you made all alone. Talk about the sound that you stretched out and say the word slowly two or three times. Then, holding up a picture of a door, say "door" without the "r" sound. Pronounce it as though you were saying "daw" and ask him how it sounded. Did he hear an "errrrr" sound when you said it? Repeat this many times, using words with the sounds either at the beginning or at the end of the word. Don't bother with words that have the sound in the middle just yet. Use pictured words, such as "rrrrat" or "rrrrain."

When you say the word without the "errrr" sound, really make it clear that it doesn't have an "errrr" sound. For example, you might say "wobin" instead of "robin." Make it a definite "wwwuh" and not an "errrr." When you feel that he can hear the differences this way, then you are ready for Step 2.

2. Without using any pictures, say a pair of words, like "robin-wobin," and ask him to tell you which one had the "errrr" sound in it. Say the words slowly, stretching out the "errrr" sound and exaggerating the word without the "errrr" sound in it. Now use words that have the sound in all three places: "*r*adio-*w*adio"; "doo*r*-daw"; "hu*rr*y-hu*ww*y." As he gets better at picking out the words with "errrr" in them, begin to say the words a little faster and a little closer together. You will be surprised how well he will tell them apart in a very short time. (Sometimes say both words with the "errrr" sound in or with the "errrr" sound left out to see if he can spot this: "run-run"; "red-red"; "wun-wun"; "wed-wed." Now he is ready for Step 3.

3. Spend a little time talking about words to make sure he knows that words are made up of sounds. Make sure he understands that there are sounds at the beginning, in the middle, and at the end of words. Explain that if a sound is at the beginning, it is the very first sound you hear. Give him a word like "run-rrrun." The "errrr" sound is at the beginning. Then try another word— "summer-summerrrr." Talk about hearing the

sound at the end. This time, explain that when the sound is at the end of a word, no other sounds come after the last sound. Now try a word with the sound in the middle—"cereal-cerrreal." Hold on to the "errrr" sound and explain that when it is in the middle, you hear the other sounds on each side of the sound you are listening for. Say words for him, and ask him whether the sound is at the beginning, in the middle, or at the end. As he improves with Step 3, you will be able to give him words that have the sound in more than one place: "river" (beginning and end); "Roger" (beginning and end); "warmer" (middle and end); "sharpener" (middle and end); "remembering" (beginning and middle); "railroad" (beginning and middle); "refrigerator" (beginning, middle, and end).

Every once in a while, give him a long word that doesn't have any "errrr" sound in it. See if he can hear that the "errrr" sound isn't there. You may play this sort of game for two or three months before he will really be able to go through all three steps and hear the sounds accurately. Even then, don't expect him to say every sound. He will probably have difficulty with some of the harder sound combinations, such as "sp" in "spoon," "sk" in "skate," "st" in "stick," "cl" in "clock," "bl" in "blue," "fl" in "fly," "gr" in "grass," and "tr" in "tree." But don't be discouraged. Just be patient and stay with it. This is one of the best ways of helping your child learn to listen. Once he learns each step, play this game for four or five minutes at a time. Never push

him or insist on having long sessions. Many one- or
two-minute games are better than one ten-minute
game with a bored or frustrated child.

Riddles. Put three or four pictures in front of your
child—a cat, a dog, a rabbit, and a horse, for
example—either on a table or the floor—and try
something like this:

> I purr when you pet me.
> I like to chase mice.
> When I sit on your lap,
> I feel warm and nice.
> What am I?

Make up your own riddles. They don't have to
rhyme, but if they do, it will be more interesting and
teach him how sounds are sometimes alike.

Remembering. This is fun for all the family. Start
out by saying "I'm going on a trip and I'm going to
take a *suitcase*." Then it is the next person's turn.
He says "I'm going on a trip and I'm going to take a
suitcase and some *soap*." (He repeats the first word
given and then adds one.) Each person in turn repeats "I'm going. . . ." naming everything in order,
then adding a new object. See how many your child
can remember. Don't say anything about winning.
That's not important. Just have fun with the game
and try to develop his remembering skills. You can
work on specific sounds at the same time if you say
that each thing you are going to take on the trip must
have a certain sound in it. In this example, I was
using words having the "s" sound. This game is fun
when you are taking a long car trip.

One More Time

The purpose of this chapter is to emphasize and explain further the ideas of *child management* and *becoming a person*. I am going into these subjects again because they are very important and because they are so often misunderstood when they are included in guides for parents.

CHILD MANAGEMENT OR DISCIPLINE?

Is child management needed? Is discipline needed? Are we talking about the same thing when we use the words "child management" and "discipline"? Let us look at what these words mean.

Child management begins in infancy, when your child first learns about limits. Think of child management as a kind of total involvement in helping your child learn about living with others. It means that he learns about rights, his own as well as those of others. Learning to respect the rights of others means learning what rules or limits are all about, what happens when you follow the rules, and what happens when you go past limits. One of the first rules or limits he will find out about is his regular bedtime. It is a rule you will want him to learn quickly, for the sake of his health and your peace of mind. Another rule he will quickly come to know concerns regular mealtimes. He will also learn the rules about playing with toys, both his own and someone else's.

As part of a child's growing and developing, he must learn that there are limits to what he is allowed to do at certain times in his life. His first limits are set for safety reasons. He must learn that he cannot play with sharp objects or touch a hot stove, because he may get cut or burned by doing so. He cannot be allowed to hurt someone else by hitting, kicking, biting, poking, pushing, or scratching when he gets angry. He may raise a fuss when he discovers these limitations, but he must learn that although he has certain rights, so do others. He must learn that he can make certain decisions. For example, he may decide not to share certain toys because they are his special toys that only he plays with. Likewise, he must come to understand that other people might have things they don't want to share—for example, his parents' little knickknacks and plants, or some of his playmates' toys. If you wish to teach the value of sharing, then teach by sharing. Use plenty of self-talk (see Glossary) to make your point. (For instance, if you are eating a cookie, you might break off a piece and as you hand it to him, say "I'm sharing my cookie with you.") Your child should also come to know that in addition to sharing objects, he must share the people in his life.

How can you, his parents, help your child learn? There are two important things to remember. They are easy to say but hard to do: (1) try to think before you act, and (2) be consistent.

Let's start with thinking before you act. When

your "terrible" two-year-old has a tantrum in a store, he may do so because he has learned that he can get what he wants by putting on a show of crying, screaming, or yelling. Think back to his infancy and his early crying. We know that crying is useful because it tells you many things about your baby. If you respond to his crying too often or too quickly, this teaches him that crying is handy for getting your attention and what he wants. So, from the beginning, pay attention to *how you respond* to his crying. The sooner he learns that there are limits to what his crying will get him, the easier your tasks in meeting his needs will be as he gets older.

Being consistent does not mean being rigid. There are general times to eat, go to bed, stay up, and play. But don't let the clock set the exact time for all of these. For instance, if your child won't eat his food at his regular mealtimes, don't force him. But then make sure he doesn't snack between meals. He may then want his next meal a little earlier than usual. That's fine. Don't make him wait those extra minutes. He will be hungry enough by then to eat his vegetables as well as his dessert. If you are consistent in answering his cries, consistent with feeding on a schedule of sorts, and consistent with his nap time and bedtime, you are starting out on the right foot of good child management.

What about discipline? In working with parents, I find that when they talk about discipline they usually use words like "spanking," "scolding," or "punishing." Words like those suggest to me that discipline means a particular way of using force to train or teach. Therefore, let us think of child management as a broad, most effective concept aiding total development, and discipline as the least effective method of aiding total development.

Parents often ask "Can my child really learn to behave as I want him to without physical punishment?" "Will child management really work?" When they raise these questions, they usually are thinking of an older child on whom punishment or force has already been used as a means of training or teaching. Positive child management *will* work. It will work best if you start it with your infant, because he has nothing to unlearn and relearn. An older child, used to punishments, will take longer in adjusting to positive child management methods, but he will adjust to them, and in time, will grow and develop with less difficulty.

I won't argue about whether you will or will not spank or yell at your child. Somewhere between his sixth month and sixteenth year (or even later!) you will, because you are human and so is he. I am most concerned about *how often* you spank, hit, or shout at him. Frequent punishment of this kind can interfere with a child's learning processes. Are you going to make his fear of you your main method of managing him? I hope not. There are far more effective ways and many authors who will share them with you. (See "Books for Parents" on page 239.) A few of these ways are outlined in this book. If you are able to keep spankings to a minimum as he grows and develops, you are well on your way to helping him learn to get along with others without using force.

BECOMING A PERSON

The kind of person a baby becomes depends a great deal on those around him, but not completely. The kind of person he will become also depends upon what he inherits from his parents. The many differences we find in people are determined partly by environment and partly by heredity. If you keep in mind that both are involved, it may help you understand him as you try to do a more effective job of being a parent.

We have often mentioned feelings, in *Teach Your Child to Talk*. Good, positive feelings between you and your child, as well as good and positive feelings about himself, are necessary in helping him prepare to face his world. Feelings are important in his learning how to talk and in his becoming the kind of person he will become.

The process of becoming a man or becoming a woman goes on most of our lives, but it has its most important beginnings in infancy and early childhood. Learning to feel good about oneself and developing self-confidence begin at birth, and depend on those closest to the person from infancy on. But remember that children have a special ability to "bounce back" or "grow up in spite of us," and that in the course of his life each child will have many opportunities to develop his given potential to the fullest.

There is no one method to help a child grow and develop because each human being is so complex and different in so many ways. This means that being flexible is an important part in the development of your skills as a parent. The information in this book is designed to be adjustable—to meet your needs as well as your child's. Remember, *Teach Your Child to Talk—A Guide for Parents* is meant to be just that—a guide. It is intended to help you learn more about "parenting," to develop and improve your parenting skills. But it is also, and especially, meant to be a help for your child. Being a parent is many things, and I hope that this book has convinced you that one of those things should be *fun*. Learning to talk, play, think, feel good about yourself, like yourself, get along with others—all these and more—can be enjoyable for both you and your child. There are many ways to help children grow and develop. This book is dedicated to the idea that all children can and should achieve vital and fulfilling lives.

APPENDIX

Recognizing Speech And Language Problems Early

There is no set schedule or timetable for growing and developing. Each person grows and develops at a rate that is right for him or her. But sometimes there are signs that tell us about possible difficulties in certain areas of growth and development. Here are some general guidelines that can help discover whether a speech or language problem is in the making.

If any of the following statements is true of your child, then I suggest that you contact your local school and ask to talk to a specialist in speech therapy. If you are not sure about how your child is doing, it will take only a little time and effort to have the following things checked out:

1. Your child is not talking *at all* by the age of two.
2. You have a difficult time understanding him after the age of three.
3. He is leaving off many beginning consonants after age three.
4. He is still not using two- to three-word sentences by age three.

5. Sounds appear more than a year late in his speech, according to the sound-development sequence on page 219.
6. His speech consists mostly of vowel sounds.
7. His word endings are usually missing after age five.
8. His sentence structure is quite faulty at age five.
9. He is embarrassed and bothered by his speech at any age.
10. He is making errors in speech sounds (other than "wh") after age seven.
11. His voice is a monotone, or is too loud or too soft, or is of a poor quality. (Any of these may indicate a hearing loss.)
12. His voice quality is too high or too low for his age and sex.
13. He sounds as if he is talking through his nose or as if he has a cold.
14. His speech is too fast, or too slow, or doesn't flow naturally after age five.

You may be worried and concerned about some aspect of your child's development. Most of us are at one time or another. If you feel any concern, it will be better for both of you if you take time to talk to someone about him. Schools are a good place to start. You may ask to see a school psychologist, a specialist in speech therapy, a social worker, or a teacher-consultant for the physically impaired. Don't hesitate to ask. These people can be contacted at many schools during most of the year, and their services are available without cost. You can also contact your local hospital or health department.

Glossary

Babbling. What is heard when a baby combines a vowel sound and a consonant sound and repeats them over and over—for example, "ga-ga-ga-ga" or "pa-pa-pa-pa." It is believed that babies babble because they enjoy the feeling. This pleasurable feeling encourages a child to repeat the syllable even more.

Baby Talk. Talking purposely done in a childish way, such as saying "Is my widdo baby weddy for din-din?" Adults should never talk this way to children. It is *not* baby talk, however, to imitate the individual sounds and syllables that a baby says, such as "eee," "dee," and "ahm."

Cerebral Palsy. The inability to control body movements, caused by nonprogressive brain damage resulting from a prenatal defect or brain injury.

Comfort Sounds. The sounds made by a baby who is feeling good. Usually made by accident, they are the result of changes in tension of the muscles used for speech. Some of the sounds will be those used in the English language, like "k," "mmm," "aah," or "nnn."

Diabetes. The most common definition of diabetes is "the condition in which the body cannot utilize sugar normally, causing unusually high sugar levels in blood and urine." The medical term is *diabetes mellitus*. The discovery and use of insulin have made the control of diabetes possible.

Epilepsy. A chronic disorder of the nervous system, characterized by sudden loss of consciousness and sometimes by convulsions. Epilepsy characterized by severe convulsions is called *grand mal;* epilepsy characterized by minor, sometimes hardly noticeable, seizures is called *petit mal*.

First Meaningful Word. A baby's first real word used with its accepted meaning. It must sound similar to the way an adult might say that word, so that if a stranger were to hear the child say it, he would be able to understand what the child means without having to interpret any of his gestures.

Hydrocephalus. (Also called *water on the brain).* An accumulation of cerebrospinal fluid within the brain.

Hypoglycemia. (Also called *low blood sugar).* An abnormally small amount of glucose in the blood, which can lead to insulin shock.

Hyperactive. A hyperactive child is extremely fussy, restless, and demanding, moves about a great deal, does not seem to like to be cuddled or comforted, has a poor sleeping schedule, takes a long time to feed, and has a short attention span.

Inflection. Inflections are caused by raising and lowering the pitch of your voice and/or raising and lowering the volume of your voice to help make the meaning of your spoken words clear.

Jargon. The use of assorted meaningless syllables. Usually it will sound as if it is something very meaningful. One explanation for jargon is that it seems to be a child's early effort to imitate the fluency of adults. Jargon is often used by children who have an inadequate vocabulary, lack the physical maturity to produce rapid adult speech, or do not understand how words can be put into meaningful sentences.

Meaningful Word. See *First Meaningful Word*.

Microcephaly. Abnormal smallness and imperfect development of the head.

Muscular Dystrophy. Any of various diseases of unknown cause, characterized by the progressive wasting away of the muscles.

Normal Nonfluency. The repetition of sounds, syllables, words, or phrases without great effort, the unnecessary prolonging of sounds and pauses, or the use of unnecessary sounds like "um" or "ah." What parents call stuttering is often *normal nonfluency*. A three-year-old child who repeats a s-s-s-sound or syl-syl-syllable like that, or a word like-like-like this is *not necessarily* a stutterer. The repeating, pauses, backing up, holding on to sounds, and general confusion of "thinking and talking" are very typical at this age.

Parallel Talk. A technique of talking out loud about what someone else is doing, seeing, hearing, or feeling at the moment. An example of parallel talk after an accident might be: "Uh-oh, Billy fell out of his wagon. Billy's crying because he scraped his knee . . . I'll bet that hurts." Parallel talk can be used (1) to help a child learn that there are words to label any object, feeling, or idea, and (2) to show how words go together to make sentences.

Self-Correction. Self-correction is just what it says. You correct mistakes that *you* make—not somebody else's.

Self-Talk. A technique of talking out loud about what

one is doing, seeing, hearing, or feeling at the moment. An example of self-talk one might use while washing the car is: "My! This car is dirty! It sure needs a good washing. I'll start washing the roof. Some of this dirt is hard to get off! Now, let's wash the windows. . . ." Through the use of self-talk, parents can expose their children to many new names and ideas as well as showing them, by example, how to put sentences together.

Spina Bifida. (Literally, a "split spine.") In the normal spine, the two sides of the back channel grow together to form the space where the spinal cord lies. In *spina bifida,* this fails to take place.

Stuttering. Speaking with involuntary pauses, spasms, and rapid repetitions of sounds, words and phrases.

Vocal Cords. (Also called *vocal folds.*) Muscle tissue in the throat, protected by a bonelike structure called the larynx (or Adam's apple; it is most prominent in men). When air is forced between this tissue, the tissue vibrates, thus producing sound.

Voice Gestures. The changes people make with their voices to give added meaning to their words. It is possible to change:

(1) the loudness
(2) the inflection (for example, "Are you tired!" contrasted with "Are you tired?")
(3) the timing (for example, "That girl said her mother is a genius" contrasted with "That girl," said her mother, "is a genius!")
(4) the pitch (high or low)
(5) the quality (breathy or nasal, for example)

Speech Sounds

From birth until age six or seven, try not to correct or criticize your child's speech and language. Many sounds are difficult to make all by themselves and even more difficult for a child to say as parts of words when he is talking. Be patient, and just be a good model for him to imitate. If you are concerned as he grows and develops, there are many people who can help you.

The person you go to for help may be called a speech correctionist, a speech therapist, or a speech pathologist. Such a person knows all about the development of children's speech and language, and will know what your child's needs are. Don't be afraid about asking for help for your child, no matter what his age.

If you feel he has trouble saying certain words, listen carefully for the sound or sounds he is having difficulty with. Compare your way of saying a word with his. Notice which sounds you both say the same way and which sounds you say differently. Don't try to correct the way he says a word by saying things like "Now, Tommy, don't say 'It's waining,' say 'It's raining.' Say it the way I do. Say 'raining.' " Instead:

1. Exaggerate the sounds you want your child to hear. Say things like "carrrrr" and "rrrrrrun."
2. Make the same errors your child makes and then correct them in your own speech.
3. Have your child look into a mirror sometimes as you and he talk. This way he will be able to see

as well as hear and feel the way different sounds are made.

Here is an important point to remember. People from various parts of the United States pronounce some sounds in a manner typical of their own area. These regional differences are not considered speech problems. There is no single "correct" way of pronouncing American English.

As children grow older, their ability to produce the more difficult sounds improves. The table of Sound Development Norms on page 219 includes an approximate age at which children should be using various sounds correctly. Keep the following points in mind as you read this section on speech sounds:

1. This section is included to help you understand how speech sounds are made. It is *not* intended to be used for drills in correcting your child's speech.

2. Don't expect your child to use any specific speech sound *before* the age mentioned in the list.

3. The table of Sound Development Norms is based on research in which a large number of children were tested at different ages. Of the children tested, 25 percent *did not* make some or all of the sounds correctly at the age shown. This means that your child will probably say some sounds differently, too, at each age level.

4. You will notice that in the lists and explanations that follow some of the sounds are marked *voiced* and some *unvoiced*. A voiced (or noisy) sound is made when air goes past the vocal

cords and causes them to vibrate. Sounds for the letters "z," "b," and "d" are voiced sounds. An unvoiced (or quiet) sound is made when air goes past the vocal cords without causing them to vibrate. Sounds for the letters "s," "p," "t," and "sh" are unvoiced sounds.

5. Following the table of Sound Development Norms is an explanation of how each sound is made. The more difficult sounds are at the end of the list. Become familiar with how each sound is made.

6. When explaining to your child how to make a particular sound, make your explanations simple.

7. *Don't try to rush your child's speech development*. It will take time. Plan for this. Don't pressure him to perform beyond his ability. If he's not ready for something, wait a while. Always remember, there is no *exact* time when your child must use a particular sound correctly. Above all, learning to make sounds and using them in words should always be fun for both you and your child.

Templin Sound Development Norms

Age	Sounds
3	mmmm, nnnn, ng, f, p, h, w
4	y, k, b, d, g, r
4½	ssss, sh, ch
6	t, v, l, th (unvoiced)
7	zzzz, zh, j, th (voiced)
8	wh

VOWEL SOUNDS

Vowel sounds are the first sounds your child uses. You can hear them during his "comfort sound" play. Most parents aid speech development automatically by imitating these early sounds. Once your child starts making comfort sounds, it is important that you make many different sounds for him to imitate. This same holds true when he begins to "babble." Starting with "mama" and "dada," you can easily go on to "me, me," "my, my," "do, do," and so forth.

As your child's listening skills develop, he will add all his vowel sounds if he hears them often enough from you. The following are examples of the basic vowel sounds he should hear:

a (*a*pple, c*a*r, g*a*me)
e (f*ee*t, t*e*n)
i (s*i*t, k*i*te)
o (g*o*, *o*ut)
u (*u*p, *u*se)

HOW SPEECH SOUNDS ARE MADE

(**Note:** The order in which the sounds are listed is the same as that for the Sound Development Norms, with the more difficult sounds at the end of the list.)

m *(mom)*
This is one of the nasal sounds, made with the soft palate (the rearmost part of the roof of the mouth) in a lowered position. Close your lips and make a humming sound through your nose.

N (*n*o)

Another of the nasal sounds, so the soft palate is lowered. With your tongue in a flattened position, press the tongue tip against the upper gum ridge of the roof of the mouth (the hard palate). Make a sound like humming, but with your lips open and your teeth slightly apart.

ng (you*ng*)

This is a nasal sound too, so again the soft palate is lowered. Arch the back of the tongue, so that it presses slightly against the rearmost portion of the roof of the mouth (the soft palate). Hold it there and hum with your mouth open.

f (*f*ood)

Bite lightly on your lower lip with your upper front teeth and blow air quietly between the lower lip and the cutting edge of the upper teeth.

p (*p*op)

Press your lips together and build up air pressure. Then quickly open them by sending out a puff of air.

h (*h*ot)

Part the teeth and lips. The tongue is down, with tip touching lightly against the lower gum ridge. As air is forced out, the tongue quickly changes to the position of the following vowel in the word.

w (*w*ood)

Round your lips as if making the sound "oo" (as in food). With the tongue slightly rolled up at the sides, allow air to pass out through the lips while the vocal cords vibrate, and quickly change to the position of the vowel sound that follows.

y (*y*es)
Widen and raise the middle part of your tongue
slightly as you make an "eee" sound. The tip of the
tongue is lowered, and the teeth are slightly sepa-
rated. While the vocal cords vibrate, change quickly
to the position of the vowel sound that follows.

k (*c*ake)
This sound is made near the back of the throat. Arch
the back of your tongue so that it presses tightly
against the rearmost portion of the roof of the mouth
(the soft palate). Build up air pressure behind your
tongue and release it quickly, as if to cough.

b (*b*oy)
The same as "p," except the vocal cords are also
made to vibrate.

d (*d*og)
With your mouth slightly open, press the tip of your
tongue on the gum ridge behind the upper teeth.
Build up air pressure behind the tongue tip. Drop
your tongue and let the air out quickly while the
vocal cords vibrate.

g (*g*o)
The same as "k," except that the vocal cords are
also made to vibrate.

r (*r*ope)
There is no single correct "r" sound. There are
many, depending on what word is said. The approximate position in most cases requires that the back of
the tongue be up close to, but not touching, the rearmost portion of the roof of the mouth (the soft palate)

and that the sides of the tongue curve up to touch lightly the upper teeth on either side. The tongue tip usually is curled slightly upward, and the sound of "eh" (as in head) is prolonged.

s (*s*oap, *c*ent)

There are two ways to produce a correct "s" sound. The most commonly used "s" is made with the tongue widened and the tip of the tongue up close to, but not touching, the upper gum ridge. The teeth are slightly apart, and air is blown down a central groove in the tongue, until a hissing sound is made by the airstream rushing between the tongue tip and the upper front teeth.

Another way of producing an "s" sound is the same as that described above, except that the tongue tip is down, slightly touching the lower gum ridge. The middle of the tongue is still up and the central groove is maintained. With this tongue position, the sharp hissing sound is made by the airstream rushing between the tongue tip and the lower front teeth.

sh (*sh*oe)

Have your tongue assume the shape for "s" first. Then round your lips as when saying "who." Now pull your tongue back a little as you push your lips forward. Blow air down the center of the tongue.

ch (*ch*air)

With your mouth slightly open and your lips rounded, have your tongue assume the shape for "d" or "t" (pressing your tongue tip against the upper gum ridge). Build up air pressure behind the tongue tip and quickly move to the "sh" position.

t (*t*oy)

The same as "d," except that the vocal cords are not made to vibrate.

v (*v*ery)

The same as "f," except that the vocal cords vibrate.

l (*l*ike)

With your mouth slightly open, broaden your tongue tip and press the tip lightly against the gum ridge behind the upper teeth. The vocal cords vibrate.

th (*th*umb)

(Unvoiced) Widen your tongue and hold it between your upper and lower teeth, so that it may be seen just slightly. Blow air over the top of your tongue, and the airstream will then hit the upper front teeth to produce the voiceless "th" sound.

z (*z*ipper)

The same as "s," except that the vocal cords vibrate.

zh (trea*s*ure)

The same as "sh," except that the vocal cords are also made to vibrate.

j (*j*ump)

The same as "ch," except that the vocal cords are also made to vibrate.

th (*th*ey)

(Voiced) The same as unvoiced "th," except that the vocal cords are also made to vibrate.

wh (*wh*ere)

(Often the voiced "w," as in wood, is substituted for this sound, and is considered correct.) Round your lips and roll your tongue up at the sides slightly. Blow air quietly between the lips.

Finger Plays

Pat-a-Cake

Pat-a-cake, pat-a-cake, baker's man, *(clap hands together lightly)*
Bake me a cake
As fast as you can.
Roll it, *(pass hands over each other in circular motion)*
And pat it, *(touch hands together lightly)*
And mark it with "B," *(use index finger as if writing letter "B")*
And bake it in the oven for baby and me. *(outstretch arms as if putting cake in oven)*

Pease Porridge Hot

Pease porridge hot; *(slap knees, clap hands, clap your hands against child's hands)*
Pease porridge cold; *(repeat)*
Pease porridge in the pot *(slap knees, clap hands, clap child's right hand with your right hand, clap hands together)*
Nine days old. *(clap child's left hand with your left hand, clap hands together, clap your hands against child's hands).*
Some like it hot; *(repeat sequence above)*
Some like it cold;
Some like it in the pot
Nine days old.

The House

This is the roof of the house so good *(make peaked roof with hands)*
These are the walls made out of wood, *(palms vertical and parallel)*
These are the windows that let in the light, *(join thumbs and index fingers)*
This is the door that shuts so tight, *(palms together)*
This is the chimney so straight and tall. *(arm up straight)*
Oh, what a good house for one and all. *(arms at angle for roof above head, one hand extending for chimney)*

Here's the Church

Here's the church;	*(fingers interlocked, palms down)*
Here's the steeple;	*(index fingers raised to a point)*
Open the door	*(keep fingers interlocked, but turn palms up)*
And see all the people.	*(wiggle fingers)*

Jack-in-the-Box

Jack-in-the box	
Sits so still.	*(hand closed, thumb inside)*
"Won't you come out?"	
"Yes! I will!"	*(thumb "jumps" out)*

Jack Be Nimble

Jack be nimble,	*(hold closed fist with thumb standing)*
Jack be quick,	
Jack jump over	*(first hand hops over second)*
The candle stick.	

Baby

Here's a ball for baby	
Big and soft and round.	*(hands form a ball)*
Here is baby's hammer,	
Oh, how he can pound!	*(pound fists)*
Here is baby's music,	
Clapping, clapping so.	*(clap hands)*
Here are baby's dollies,	
Standing in a row.	*(hold fingers up)*
Here is baby's trumpet,	
Too too toot, too too.	*(hands form horn)*

Peep In

Peep in,	*(touch eyelids)*
Lift up the latch	*(tip of Nose)*
Walk in;	*(touch lips)*
And take a little chair.	*(tuck finger in neck)*

Ten Little Fingers

I have ten little fingers,
And they all belong to me.
I can make them do things—
Would you like to see?
I can put them up high,
I can put them down low,
I can make them hide,
And I can fold them just so.

Hands

Open them and shut them,
Open them and shut them,
Open them and shut them,
And give a little clap.

Open them and shut them,
Open them and shut them,
Open them and shut them,
And put them in your lap.

Creepy, creepy, creepy,
Up to your chin,
Open your mouth and
Pop them in!

Me

My hands upon my head I place,
On my shoulder, on my face,
On my knees, and at my side,
Then I raise them up SO high,
Swiftly count to 1, 2, 3,
And see how quiet they can be.
(bring hands down slowly and place them in lap)

Little Miss Muffet

Little Miss Muffet	*(thumb straight up)*
Sat on a tuffet,	
Eating her curds and whey.	*(eating motion with other hand)*
Along came a spider	*(twirling fingers from high)*
And sat down beside her	*(down toward thumb)*
And frightened Miss Muffet away.	*(as spider fingers reach thumb, quickly put thumb behind back)*

Teensy, Weensy Spider

A teensy, weensy spider	
Climbed up the water spout.	*(fingers climb upward atop each other)*
Down came the rain	*(wiggle fingers to make rain)*
And washed the spider out.	*(hands and arms flung downward and outward)*
Out came the sun	*(hands form circle)*
And dried up all the rain,	*(hands open wide and outward)*
And the teensy, weensy spider	
Climbed up the spout again.	*(fingers climb upward as before)*

The Firemen

Ten brave firemen	*(ten fingers straight up)*
Sleeping in a row.	*(fingers out flat)*
Ding! Goes the bell!	*(clap hands)*
Down the pole they go.	*(motion of going down a pole)*
Jumping on the engine,	*(motion of driving)*
Oh! Oh!	*(hands shaped like hose; hissing noises like water)*
Putting out the fire.	
Back home so slow,	*(driving motion, slow)*
All in a row.	

Fall Leaves

Leaves are floating softly down;   *(arms raised, fingers*
They make a carpet on the ground;   *wiggling; gradually*
                                                    lower to the floor)

When, swish! The wind comes whirling by   *(move both arms*
                                                    quickly from one
                                                    side to the other)

And sends them dancing to the sky.   *(wiggle fingers and*
                                                    arms in the air)

The Flowers

When the flowers are thirsty,   *(both hands form cup,*
                                                    representing flowers)

And the grass is dry,   *(hands spread out flat)*
Merry little raindrops   *(hands and fingers coming*
Tumble from the sky.   *from sky like raindrops)*
All around they patter   *(fingers tapping on floor*
In their happy play,   *or table)*
Till the little sunbeams   *(hands and arms form a*
Chase them all away.   *round sun)*

Birds Flying

Up, up in the sky   *(fingers flying like birds)*
The little birds fly,
Down, down in the nest,   *(hands form nest)*
The little birds rest,
With a wing on the left,   *(hands on each hip)*
And a wing on the right.
Let the little birds rest   *(head to one side as if*
All the long night.   *tucking under wing)*

Helping Mother

I help my mother.	
I sweep the floor,	*(swing arms pretending to sweep)*
I dust the table,	*(make a circular motion with one hand)*
I run to the store,	*(run a few steps, then run back)*
I help her beat eggs,	*(hold hands together, moving one in a small circle)*
And sift the flour for cakes.	*(holding one hand closed, shake it back and forth)*
Then I help her eat	
All the good things she makes.	*(holds hand to lips, pretending to take a bite of something)*

Little Boy

This little boy is going to bed;	*(index finger on right hand is boy)*
Down on the pillow he lays his head,	*(thumb of left hand on edge of left palm forms pillow)*
Wraps himself in the covers so tight.	*(fingers of left hand close over index finger of right hand as blankets)*
There he stays all the long night.	
Morning comes; he opens his eyes.	
Back with a toss the covers fly.	*(fingers of left hand open up)*
Up he jumps, he's off and away,	*(index finger of right hand jumps up)*
Ready for work and ready for play.	

Jack-o'-Lanterns

Five little Jack-o'-Lanterns sitting on a gate:	*(fingers on one hand held up and spread out)*
This one said, "My, it's getting late!"	*(take hold of thumb)*
This one said, "Who goes there?"	*(second finger)*
This one said, "There are Brownies in the air!"	*(third finger)*
This one said, "Let's run, let's run!"	*(fourth finger)*
This one said, "Oh, it's only Halloween fun."	*(fifth finger)*
Puff! Went the wind, out went the lights,	*(hands clap for "puff")*
Away went the Jack-o'-Lanterns On Halloween night.	*(hands behind back)*

The Turkey

"Gobble, gobble," says the turkey.	*(right fist forms body, left fingers form tail; thumb on right hand stuck out is turkey's head)*
"Soon will be Thanksgiving day. Would you eat me? How you treat me! I will run away."	*(hands behind back)*

Books And Records

GETTING ACQUAINTED WITH BOOKS

Take your four-year-old youngster to the children's room at the public library. Prepare him for the trip by talking about this room. Tell him that it is a special place for children just like him, and that he can look at books there. When you arrive, he will probably find it strange, so give him time to take it all in slowly.

Show him the picture books and help him pick one or two and take them to one of the little tables. He can sit there and leaf through the books quietly. Use your library card to take out his favorite book of the group and let him carry it home. It's an important day, this first one at the library. Let him talk about it at home to the rest of the family.

Many libraries have a children's librarian. She will be glad to help both of you find books that are right for your child. She may also offer you a book list or tell you about books covering a wide range of children's literature. Perhaps the library has a preschool story hour to which you may take your child. Notice how the librarian involves the children when she talks about the book that is being read at the story hour. Stay to listen. You may be able to pick up some useful hints on reading children's books aloud.

Try to visit a bookstore or the book section in a department store. If you can, let your child choose a book—with your help, of course. Or perhaps he can look forward to getting a book that he has seen there when Christmas, a birthday, or some other special occasion rolls around. A possible choice for his first real book might be a Mother Goose or a book of animal stories.

Note: For additional information, you may want to consult this book:

> *A Parent's Guide to Children's Reading,* by Nancy Larrick
> Hard-cover: Doubleday and Company, Inc.
> Paperback: Bantam Books

Many books chosen for the list on the following pages were recommended by this guide. It gives titles, content description, and suggested age level for many more books, and contains much additional useful information besides.

BOOKS FOR CHILDREN

Here is a list of children's books, organized by age level, with comments on special interests. It gives titles, publishers, and, usually, authors. You may find these books in libraries, bookstores, book departments of department stores, or even in drug stores, variety stores, or supermarkets. You may wish to buy some of these books. While it is true that libraries have great riches in the way of children's books, your child will want to have his very own book or books, too. Perhaps *you* can remember a special, dog-eared book that was once very important to you in the years before you went to school.

If you cannot find a book you want at your local bookstore, ask them to order it for you. They will tell you the price of the book, and whether there are shipping charges or other additional charges.

Six to Twelve Months

At eight or nine months, a baby will delight in listening to simple nursery rhymes. He enjoys the old games such as "This little pig went to market" and "Pat-a-cake." Nursery rhymes have very little plot but a child is intrigued by their repetition and rhythm. Remember, a lot of lap-time spent looking at books will help your child associate books with fun and good times. Learning to like books starts now.

Baby's Book of Animals, James & Jonathan, Inc. Ideal for six-month-old child. Colorful pictures; pages not easily torn. Available in retail outlets.

What the Animals Say, James & Jonathan, Inc. Cloth picture book with brief text; good pictures. Available in retail outlets.

Baby Animals Board Book, illustrated by Gyo Fujikawa, McLoughlin Brothers.

Farm Animals Board Book, illustrated by Irma Wilde, McLoughlin Brothers.

Baby's Mother Goose, illustrated by Alice Schlesinger, McLoughlin Brothers. Colorful pictures; simple, suitable content.

Tall Book of Mother Goose, The, illustrated by Feodor Rojankovsky, Harper and Row. The bold colors of the pictures are attractive to youngsters.

Real Mother Goose, The, illustrated by Blanche Fisher Wright, Rand McNally. Appealing pictures.

One to Two Years

When your child is twelve to eighteen months old, try bedtime stories. Put your arm around him, share a book, and enjoy a warm, wonderful time.

(Sometimes your child may not want you to read to him, or the book you have chosen may not be suitable. Respect his choice.)

Come Walk With Me; I Look Out My Window; This Is My House; My Toys; Let's Go Shopping; A Trip to the Zoo; designed by Aurelius Battaglia, Playskool Play Books, Playskool Manufacturing Company, Inc. These books are available only at retail outlets.

Baby Farm Animals, by Garth Williams, Golden Press. Just a few words of text—and charming pictures. The pages are made of strong cardboard.

Child's Good Night Book, A, by Margaret Wise Brown, illustrated by Jean Charlot, Addison-Wesley. A thoroughly satisfying book, and one that may be a calming preliminary to going to bed.

Goodnight Moon, by Margaret Wise Brown, illustrated by Clement Hurd, Harper and Row. Part of the fun of this book is locating the mouse in each picture.

Two to Three Years

The two-year-old youngster still likes the old nursery rhymes and tales. Old favorites are still welcome, but at the same time he wants to learn more about the world around him. He learns by experience—and from books too.

Tall Book of Nursery Tales, The, illustrated by Feodor Rojankovsky, Harper and Row. Twenty-four simply told, familiar tales with realistic illustrations.

Johnny Crow's Garden, by L. Leslie Brooke, illustrated by the author, Frederick Warne. Handsome pictures. The fascinating feathered or furred animal faces tell more than the few words of the text.

Ask Mr. Bear, by Marjorie Flack, Macmillan. Beautifully illustrated surprise picture book, available in hard-cover and paperback editions.

One Bright Monday Morning, by Arline and Joseph Baum, Random House.

We Went Looking, by Aileen Fisher, illustrated by Marie Angel, Crowell.

Three to Four Years

A three- to four-year-old is able to sit still for longer periods of time, and will like longer stories. Talk to him about what's happening in the stories you read, to add to his expressive language skills.

Golden Counting Book, The, by Roberta Miller, illustrated by Robert J. Lee, Golden Press.

Kittens, Puppies, Horses, Rabbits, Turtles, and Birds, by Cynthia Iliff Koehler and Alvin Koehler, Grosset & Dunlap, Inc. A redesigned combination of nine earlier Wonder Books. You may wish to consider it a limited sort of "pre-encyclopedia."

All Falling Down, by Gene Zion, illustrated by Margaret Bloy Graham, Harper and Row.

Beady Bear, by Don Freeman, illustrated by the author, Viking.

Best Friends for Frances, by Russell Hoban, illustrated by Lillian Hoban, Harper and Row.

Camel Who Took a Walk, The, by Jack Tworkov, illustrated by Roger Duvoisin, Dutton. Available in hardcover and paperback editions.

Friend Is Someone Who Likes You, A, by Joan Walsh Anglund, Harcourt Brace Jovanovich.

Letter to Amy, A, by Ezra Jack Keats, illustrated by the author, Harper and Row.

Millions of Cats, by Wanda Gag, illustrated by the author, Coward, McCann and Geoghegan. Told in folk-tale style, ornamented with wood-block pictures. Children love the repetition of the chant, "Hundreds of cats, thousands of cats, millions and billions and trillions of cats."

Play With Me, by Marie Hall Ets, illustrated by the author, Viking.

Peter's Chair, by Ezra Jack Keats, illustrated by the author, Harper and Row.

Four to Five Years

Four- and five-year-old children still enjoy nursery rhymes and tales. Now they like reciting them or telling you part of the story. Animal stories are still very popular, but instead of being interested in the more familiar cats, dogs, and other domestic animals, they now want to hear about other animals, such as lions, elephants, bears, or camels.

Amelia Bedelia, by Peggy Parish, illustrated by Fritz Siebel, Harper and Row. Story of Amelia who followed directions—literally—with funny results. Shows how words can be combined to mean something more than the meaning of each separate word.

Anatole, by Eve Titus, illustrated by Paul Galdone, McGraw-Hill. Story of a mouse who is chief taster at a cheese factory.

Caps for Sale, by Esphyr Slobodkina, illustrated by the author, Addison-Wesley.

Curious George, by H. A. Rey, illustrated by the author, Houghton Mifflin. Part of series popular with children; about a mischievous monkey who gets into all kinds of trouble.

Five Chinese Brothers, The, by Claire Huchet Bishop, illustrated by Kurt Wiese, Coward, McCann and Geoghegan.

Flip, by Wesley Dennis, illustrated by the author, Viking.

Fun for Chris, by Blossom Randall, illustrated by Eunice Young Smith, Whitman.

Happy Lion, The, by Louise Fatio, illustrated by Roger Duvoisin, McGraw-Hill. A lion escapes from the zoo to see the world.

Horton Hatches the Egg, by Dr. Seuss (Theodore Seuss Geisel), illustrated by the author, Random House. Youngsters like the outlandish pictures and rhymes of all the Dr. Seuss books.

Little House of Your Own, A, by Beatrice Schenk de Regniers and Irene Haas, Harcourt Brace Jovanovich.

Lollipop Party, The, by Ruth A. Sonneborn, illustrated by Brinton Turkle, Viking.

Make Way for Ducklings, by Robert McCloskey, illustrated by the author, Viking. Especially satisfying story with warm, amusing drawings.

Nine Days to Christmas, by Marie Hall Ets and Aurora Labastida, illustrated by Marie Hall Ets, Viking.

Richard Scarry's Best Word Book Ever, by Richard Scarry, illustrated by the author, Golden Press. Words are grouped around children's activities.

Snowy Day, The, by Ezra Jack Keats, illustrated by the author, Viking. Charming pictures, simple text.

Switch on the Night, by Ray Bradbury, illustrated by Madeleine Gekiere, Pantheon Books.

Theodore Turtle, by Ellen MacGregor, illustrated by Paul Galdone, McGraw-Hill.

Umbrella, by Taro Yashima, illustrated by the author, Viking. To have an umbrella but no rain? A sad situation!

Very Special House, A, by Ruth Krauss, illustrated by Maurice Sendak, Harper and Row. Freedom and security are combined as the pleasures of a little boy whose "special house" is right in the middle of his head. Good for chanting in chorus with your child.

While Susie Sleeps, by Nina Schneider, Addison-Wesley.

White Snow, Bright Snow, by Alvin Tresselt, illustrated by Roger Duvoisin, Lothrop, Lee and Shepard. Describes the seasons.

Hi, Mr. Robin, by Alvin Tresselt, Lothrop, Lee and Shepard.

At this age many children become interested in machines, trains, planes, boats, and spaceships. The following books will appeal to them:

Airplanes and Trucks and Trains, Fire Engines, Boats and Ships, Building and Wrecking Machines, by George J. Zaffo, Grosset and Dunlap.

Little Toot, by Hardie Gramatky, illustrated by the author, Putnam. All about a little tugboat that gets into trouble in New York Harbor.

Little Train; Little Auto; Little Airplane; by Lois Lenski, illustrated by the author, Walck. Simple text appeals to children; illustrations are somewhat old-fashioned.

Mike Mulligan and His Steam Shovel, by Virginia L. Burton, illustrated by the author, Houghton Mifflin.

BOOKS FOR PARENTS

For additional information about early child development, we suggest a variety of books. These are listed below according to the topics they cover.

Speech and Language Development

Getting Your Baby Ready to Talk. A correspondence course for parents of very young children (six to eighteen months of age). As soon as your baby is born, write and request an application from: The John Tracy Clinic, Home Study Plan, 806 West Adams Blvd., Los Angeles, Calif. 90007.

Child Development in General

Your Baby's First Year, Children's Bureau Publication #400; 50¢

Your Child From 1 to 3, Children's Bureau Publication #413; 35¢

Your Child From 3 to 4, Children's Bureau Publication #446; 45¢

These short picture pamphlets are designed for quick and easy reading. They cover very important points parents need to consider during a child's preschool years. Order from: Superintendent of Documents, United States Government Printing Office, Washington, D.C. 20402.

Your Child From 1 to 6, Children's Bureau Publication #30; $1.10. Describes the growth of children from 1 to 6 years of age and emphasizes the child's emotional needs and his relationship to other members of the family. Order from: Superintendent of Documents, United States Government Printing Office, Washington, D.C. 20402.

Your Child From 6 to 12, Children's Bureau Publication #324; $1.15. Brings together the opinions of many specialists on how parents may help their children mature as healthy, well-adjusted, and socially responsible human beings. Order from: Superintendent of Documents, United States Government Printing Office, Washington, D.C. 20402.

Child Behavior, by F. L. Ilg and L. B. Ames, Harper and Row (paperback).

The Phenomena of Early Development, published by Ross Laboratories, Columbus, Ohio 43216. Often given away free by pediatricians.

How-to-do-it Books on Raising Children

Between Parent and Child: New Solutions to Old Problems, by Haim Ginott, Macmillan.

A Creative Life for Your Children, by Margaret Mead, Children's Bureau Headliner Series #1; 90¢. This was the heart of the theme of the Golden Anniversary White House Conference on Children and Youth. In this pamphlet, Margaret Mead, with insight and sensitivity, elaborates this theme. Order from: Superintendent of Documents, United States Government Printing Office, Washington, D.C. 20402.

A Doctor Discusses the Preschool Child's Learning and How Parents Can Help, by S. L. Warner and E. B. Rosenberg, Budlong Press Company (paperback). May be available through your doctor.

How to Raise Children at Home in Your Spare Time, by M. J. Gersh, M.D., Stein & Day (paperback). Words from a pediatrician with a sense of humor.

Infant Care, Children's Bureau Publication #8; $1.00. Designed to help mothers and fathers take care of their babies, and especially a first baby. Its advice is based on the experience of doctors, nurses, nutritionists, psychologists, and parents. *Infant Care* was first published in 1914. It is now in its eleventh edition. Order from: Superintendent of Documents, United States Government Printing Office, Washington, D.C. 20402.

Physical Coordination Skills

Success Through Play, by Don H. Radler and Newell C. Kephart, Harper and Row. Explains how to help your child develop good visual-motor skills.

Sex Education

A Teacher's Guide to Sex Education, by Winifred Kempton, Duxbury Press, North Scituate, Mass.

All About You: A Curriculum Guide on Human Growth and Development for Children with Development Disabilities, by LeeAnn Lipke, published by the Grand Rapids Public Schools System, Grand Rapids, Michigan. A book for parents and teachers. Explains how to help young children begin building positive self-concepts and self-awareness. Also a good source for books for parents on human sexuality.

Children with Special Problems

The Child With a Speech Problem, Children's Bureau Folder #52; 45¢

The Mentally Retarded Child at Home, Children's Bureau Publication #374; $1.10.

The Preschool Child Who Is Blind, Children's Bureau Folder #39; 45¢

Your Gifted Child, Children's Bureau Publication #371; 55¢.

Order all of the above from: Superintendent of Documents, United States Government Printing Office, Washington, D.C. 20402.

Communicating with Parents of Exceptional Children, by Roger L. Kroth, Love Publishing Company, Denver, Colo. While intended primarily for educators, this is an excellent source of selected readings for parents of exceptional children.

RECORDS FOR CHILDREN

This section offers a list of records for children. It includes the following information: title (and sometimes the artist); label and number or code number. In addition, it usually includes: size (10 or 12 inches); revolutions per minute (LP, equal to 33 rpm, or 78 rpm); and sometimes whether the record is monaural or stereophonic.

Records can be ordered through your local record shops or possibly borrowed from the public library.

All records in print can be ordered from: Children's Music Center, Inc., 5373 West Pico Blvd., Los Angeles, Calif. 90019.

Title/Artist	Number	Other Information
American Game and Activity Songs for Children	Folkways (3–63) 7002	12″ mono
Animal Rhythms, by Phoebe James	PJ 1	10″ 78 rpm
Animal Rhythms with Sound Effects, by Phoebe James	PJ 3	10″ 78 rpm
Circus Comes to Town, The, by Tom Glazer	Young People's 10015	mono
Child's World of Sound	CB 8	12″ LP

Note: Books to accompany the above record can be order ordered:

The Loudest Noise in the World	(BB8B)
Do You Hear What I Hear?	(B499)
Listen to My Seashell	(C601A)

Basic Concept Songs of Self-Image #1	EC 3	12″ LP
Body Concept Songs #3	EC 14	12″ LP
Color Concepts	CB 28	12″ LP
Sights and Sounds; Feeling and Perceiving	CB 36	12″ LP
Counting Games and Rhythms for the Little Ones	Folkways 7056	12″ LP
Creepy, the Crawly Caterpillar	CY 5	12″ LP
Daddy Comes Home	C 601A	12″ LP
Do You Know How You Grow Inside?	C 734	10″ LP

Title/Artist	Number	Other Information
Do You Know How You Grow Outside?	C 735	10" LP
Eensie Beensie Spider and *Skittery Skattery*	C 12	12" LP
Farm Animals	PJ 13	
Favorite Action Songs, by Phoebe James	PJ 12	10" 78 rpm
Finger Plays	CE 9A	12" LP
Five Senses, told by Marni Nixon and Donald Murphy	Bowmar (CL9) CB9	12" LP

Note: Books to accompany the above record can be ordered:

My Bunny Feels Soft	(BB9)
Do You Move as I Do?	(BB9A)
Grandfather and I	(BB9B)

Listening Time Series, by Scott and Wood		
Listening Time #1	C 213	12" LP
Listening Time #2	C 214	12" LP
Listening Time #3	C 215	12" LP
Lullabies for Sleepyheads	Camden CAL-1003	mono or stereo
Muffin in the City and *Muffin in the Country*	C 114 A	12" LP

Note: Books to accompany the above record can be ordered:

City Noisy Book	(B41)
Country Noisy Book	(B42)

Title/Artist	Number	Other Information
Noisy and Quiet; Big and Little	EC 7	12" LP
Nothing to Do	CY 12	12" LP
Nursery Rhymes, Games and Folk Songs, by Cisco Houston	Folkways TC 7006	10" LP stereo

Title/Artist	Number	Other Information
Nursery School Rhythms	PJ 21	10" 78 rpm
Out of Doors; Castle in the Sand; I Am a Circus	CY 205	LP
Pussycat's Christmas	C 254	78 rpm Book and record
Rhythms and Game Songs for the Little Ones, Vol. 2, by Ella Jenkins	Folkways 7057	12" LP
Romper Room—Songs and Games	Golden (2-61) 61	12" mono or stereo
Sleep Time Songs and Stories, by Pete Seeger	Folkways (7-58) 7525	12" mono or stereo
Sleepy Heads—Lullabies, by Dorothy Olsen	C 157	12" LP
This is Rhythm, by Ella Jenkins	Folkways 7652	12" LP

Index